THEY HAVE

REVELATION

ABSOLUTELY WRONG

THEY HAVE

REVELATION

ABSOLUTELY WRONG

Brother Fred

author**HOUSE**®

AuthorHouse™
1663 Liberty Drive
Bloomington, IN 47403
www.authorhouse.com
Phone: 1-800-839-8640

Published by AuthorHouse 01/30/13

ISBN: 978-1-4918-5802-8 (sc)
ISBN: 978-1-4918-5801-1 (e)

Library of Congress Control Number: 2014901824

This book is a work of non-fiction. Unless otherwise noted, the author and the publisher make no explicit guarantees as to the accuracy of the information contained in this book and in some cases, names of people and places have been altered to protect their privacy.

Any people depicted in stock imagery provided by Thinkstock are models, and such images are being used for illustrative purposes only. Certain stock imagery © Thinkstock.

This book is printed on acid-free paper.

Because of the dynamic nature of the Internet, any web addresses or links contained in this book may have changed since publication and may no longer be valid. The views expressed in this work are solely those of the author and do not necessarily reflect the views of the publisher, and the publisher hereby disclaims any responsibility for them.

How important is your eternal life to you? If you are a Christian & are not paying attention to the signs of the times something is wrong. You hear we are in the last days & Christ could come at any time. NO HE CAN'T because certain things MUST happen first. The book of Revelation has been a mystery for 2,000 years, but now is being revealed. What the Scholars have written & preached "IS" wrong & your life is at stake also. NO lukewarm, casual, average, mediocre Christian will make Heaven period. You're either; "ALL IN; OR YOU'RE NOT IN AT ALL". You will get the New Earth after you suffered through the Great Tribulation, which is also Hell on Earth. Did you know ALL COME OUT OF HELL? It's plainly written in Rev 20:13. That's just "1" of the things they have wrong. This book proves "man's schools can NOT teach Gods mysteries". Don't put anyone in charge of your eternal life & death! If you take going to hell lightly you ignoring what Jesus said; "Cut off you hand & foot & pluck out your eye to keep from going there".

I am not a scholar, but God rarely ever used them. They chose to IGNORE the Holy Spirit as the real teacher & go to man's schools where they can get the "Praise of men" when they come out. "What is highly esteemed among men is an abomination to God". This book is in layman's language & you will understand it. I have read their books & heard their teachings on Rev and I tell you they are wrong 90+% of the time. Some of these scholars I personally love & know most are truly saved. But Rev. they have wrong, & it broke my heart. The reason they have THIS book wrong is written in Rev & I show it in this book. They were never supposed to deal with this book. God had people in His plan to explain it in His time-line. 5 of these 100 + events in Rev are cloudy even to me.

"INTRODUCTION"

This book is only for those who care enough to study the Bible for themselves & not let their eternal life be in someone else's hands. When you see me say you get OUT of hell & it shows a scripture confirming it, don't you wonder what else they taught that may be wrong also. No Church ever preached this. Many Christians are serious loving people who just never thought their leaders can get things wrong because of the degrees they have from human schools. That's the problem; man's schools can NOT teach Gods mysteries! This may sound harsh but when a person goes to human schools to learn about a God who says Himself; "He is the teacher "they are saying; "get out the way Holy Spirit I'm going where a piece of paper from a human school will get me the praise of man & money and prestige", just like the Pharisees of old. I will only give one scripture on this 1 John 2:27; "Teaches you all things & you need NOT any man teach you." When I teach I tell my class "you only need me till you learn to follow the leading of the Spirit". Many never learn and it's not Gods fault. My goal is not to put down higher learning, <u>God controls to who His mysteries are revealed.</u> Not whoever can afford a college. College does not qualify a person on Rev. or any prophesy of the Bible.

I read a book that has every verse of Rev. in it like mine does here. Theirs has the comments of ALL the big name scholars of today who give their seal of approval on each event. The book is called "Revelation: Gods Word for the Biblically Inept". Please get it if you can and compare this with theirs. When I, teach I BRING their book to class. This way they can see the views of scholars. I have no fear they will see things their way because I have numerous scriptures to prove the truth. Their interpretations are from human wisdom. Following false teaching will not be excused at the Judgment Seat of Christ; another thing they have wrong. "If the blind lead blind BOTH fall". "My sheep hear My voice & a stranger they will not follow". "Many false prophets come and deceive many". Pastors should have stayed on Salvation & living right & left Revelation alone. Rev. 14 will show God already has certain people to reveal its mysteries. They shouldn't get mad and envious because these chosen are here to help us all.

Consider this; if you had said something for 30 years then found out you were wrong, would go before all those people and admit it lowering your pride? What if you knew their very life depended on what you had said? You will see most Pastors would rather take their whole flock to hell with them, than let their ego and degrees be put to shame. Look at Jim Jones. Churches today have way more members than 900. It won't be Kool-Aid that kills them, but a hell fire. "You can't put new wine in old bottles". So if you have not been completely taken in by traditions of these denominational Churches, you will understand this books point. Yes it will at first seem crazy as you read, but if you keep reading you will see the whole picture. Rev. is for NOW. God will not let the world end before all know the mysteries of Rev. Many Preachers hope it will end before they are exposed. I'll stop here & let the Holy Spirit that's in all believers guide you. Learn to know how He leads so you can STOP following the crowd that's on the "Broad Road".

Contents

    There are 22 Chapters in the book of Revelation & there are 22 Chapters in this book. Each Chapter in this book coincides with that Chapter in Revelation, with all the events of that Chapter explained. So if you ever wonder about a certain event you can go that Chapter & re-read that event with the scriptures backing them. I added Bible Studies I wrote "over the years" mostly on the Last Days and "inserted them as" they were first written. 2 are in the front before the Chapters begin and 9 are at the end after the Chapters.

This Book Is Harsh, Like The Book John Ate In Rev 10:9-11 "It Made His Belly Bitter. Revelation Is A Joyful Book For Those Who Get The Gospel Right. If We Get It Wrong We Are "Not" Hearing Jesus Voice. Most Will Get Their Feelings Hurt At The "Jugdment Seat Of Christ" Like Those In Matt. 7 Who Did The "Wonderful Works?" When Jesus Said; "This People Draws Nigh To Me Their Mouth & Honors Me With Their Lips, But Their Heart Is "Far" From Me". Can You Just Maybe Be One Of Them? Ezekiel 9:4 "Set A Mark On Them That Sigh And Cry [Sad & Disgusted] At The Abominations That Be Done In This Place [Temple]. If You See Nothing Wrong With 90+ % Of Religious Worship Today You Are Not Hearing The Holy Spirit. Jesus Said Himself Of These Las Days; "Many False Preachers Will Come And Deceive Many". You Have Pure Scripture Here And The Holy Spirit To Guide You. Let's Double Check What We Believe While There's Still Time.

"ALL IN; OR *NOT* IN AT ALL"
Luke Chapter 14

This title tells the whole story. If you are not a 100% Christian, you will not be considered a Christian at all according to what Jesus says. If you endured to the end "IN" the right doctrine & doing the right works you will make Heaven. It will be decided at the "JUDGMENT SEAT OF CHRIST" 1 CORIN. 5:10-11 & ROMANS 14:10. This is a subject Churches & Pastors stay away from because they don't know it PLUS they don't want to scare off their members with the truth. But there is ABSOLUTELY NO WAY AROUND THIS, no matter how much we wish it was not true. Most would rather hear of God's love & no one is perfect. So let's see what Jesus says AGAIN & if you will accept it or not. John 12: 48 "... the words I speak shall judge you."

Luke 14 the whole chapter gives us some ABSOLUTES about who will be His & who will NOT. Before you say it's too hard to do remember; "greater is He in us"; "we are more than conquers"; Rev. 12:11 "loved not lives unto death".....etc. *Rev. 21:27 only ones who can go IN the Holy City are those names still in Christ's book of life. I say STILL because Rev. 3:5 says Jesus will BLOT some names out HIS BOOK". How many of you knew just like your name goes IN it can come OUT!!!!!!*

1. Luke 14:8-11; Pride & high-mindedness & self-glory are the condition of these. We are told to be humble, self-sacrificing

as He was. Prov. 6:16-18 the # 1 thing God hates is "A PROUD LOOK". What causes pride; riches- certain race issues- need to be better than others. *NO HEAVEN!!*

2. Luke 14:12-14; Helping & purposefully going to POOR. Most Churches today don't even want poor members, nor reach out to them. Neither do their members. Compare the works of those Christians in Matt. 7:22-23 who were REJECTED to those who got IN, in Matt. 25: 34-35 they dealt with, helped, purposely reached out to the poor who could NOT pay back.

3. Luke 14:15-20; Jesus speaks clearly now on those who will be married to Him in Heaven at the Supper. *REMEMBER THERE WILL BE A NEW EARTH FOR THOSE WHO MISS HEAVEN!!!* Notice the first 2 excuses. Problem is they have too much money. Most were poor & owned NO land, let alone an ox; & he had 5 oxen. Seed on Thorns says; "...deceitfulness of riches chokes word & he is unfruitful". That's what happened to these. Next guy thinks he has perfect excuse; he just got married!! Verse 26 Jesus covers that also. *NO EXCUSE FOR ANY REASON WILL WORK AT ALL!!*

4. Luke 14:21-24; Notice how angry Jesus is about their so-called excuses to put HEAVEN & HIM who died for them in 2nd & 3rd place. He says [forget them forever] Go get the poor, cripple, blind, street people. These amount to the homeless, whores, criminals, druggies etc who WILL accept Him & be saved at the last time. These have no riches etc to stop them from HIS work. Match this with Matt. 21:31 "...sinners & whores go to Heaven before you...". Plus these are the "Last that will be FIRST"; MATT. 20:16 & 19:30 & 22;14!!!

LET ME SPEAK ON REPLACEMENT THEOLOGY SOME WOULD USE HERE. Yes Jesus was speaking to the Jews under the Law. We are the new Jews Romans 2:28-29. If not we would have to forget all He said to them. It is for US now; Christians who do the same & be lost.

5. Luke 14:26-27 Hate means if it comes to it you WILL drop your loved ones in a hot minute to stay with Christ & His work. Matt. 10:36; "...a man's foes WILL be they of his OWN household...". Verse 27; Cross means death period. "WE" see beforehand this may very well happen to us & we accept it. Rev. 12:11 "...they loved not their lives unto the death...". "...he who will save his life WILL lose it"[anyway]. So most of us REAL Christians will not be killed, BUT if it comes we accept it.

6. Luke 14:28-30; "Tower" used here is NO accident. He did say a house. A tower is extreme & so are His true followers. All will know you & who you work for. You cannot hide at all. We are not "Lukewarm" like those who will be spit OUT. Lukewarm is average; casual, mediocre. *NO HEAVEN!!*

7. LUKE 14:31-32; this tells us we are going against a greater number. We are in the minority. That will scare off most by itself. But not Real Christians!!!!

8. Luke14:33 "FORSAKE ALL" it's the 3rd time in 8 verses He says *"CAN NOT BE MY DISCIPLE".* Which means; they will not make Heaven period. 1/2 steppers, some-timey, casual, fair weathersWill not make Heaven at all case closed. No matter what your Preachers says. Believe Jesus!!

9. Luke 14:33-35; Jesus said we are the salt of the earth. If we lose our Saltiness we are good for nothing but to be THROWN OUT. And ALL who don't do ALL He said WILL be thrown out [back] Like the "Goats'; Tares; Lazy Servant; Lukewarm etc.

IF YOU ARE NOT READY TO BE OUT NUMBERED; HATED OF ALL; WORK; DEAL WITH POOR; HUMBLE YOURSELF; EVEN DIE, YOU ARE NOT A TOWER, NOR WILL MAKE HEAVEN. WE CAN WIN THIS CROWN WITH FLYING COLORS. HEAVEN IS WORTH IT. STOP

BEING FOOLED & FOOLING YOURSELF. GOD SPEAKS IN ABSOLUTES. "NO EXCUSES" *YOU'RE EITHER;*

"ALL IN; OR NOT IN AT ALL"!!

".. &; A SIDE ORDER OF CHRIST"

Revelation 3:16

When eating out we have a main course and even our appetizers and desserts are special to us. But we sometimes see something else on the menu we want also, so we get it as a SIDE ORDER. That side order is not the most enjoyable part of our meal, but we like it also. It's just a small part of our dining experience. This is why I am referring to Rev. 3:16 where it speaks of LUKE WARM Christians being spit out of Christ. It's the Church of Laodicea. Lukewarm means without enthusiasm or excitement. Just as that SIDE ORDER at dinner. Many Christians are just saved but without the passion and fire and excitement, and are casual, that Christ requires to make Heaven. When we see a hot passionate Christian working, studying & witnessing we say; *"it don't take all that"*. And they are called FANATICS. So let's look at a dozen scriptures on this subject to see if there will be a different reward for the MAIN COURSE CHRISTIANS, THAN THE SIDE ORDER ONES!!

1. 2 CORIN. 5:15; "...THEY LIVE NOT FOR THEMSELVES". IF YOUR PLANS AND GOALS IN LIFE ARE JOB, FAMILY, MATERIAL GAIN, SUCCESS, FAME ETC, AND THEN YOU ARE LIVING FOR YOURSELF AND CHRIST IS ONLY A *"SIDE ORDER IN YOUR LIFE"*.

2. MATT.13:44-46 "....SELLS ALL & BUYS WHOLE FIELD OR PEARL". AFTER THIS PERSON IS SAVED NOTHING ELSE IN LIFE MEANS MORE TO HIM THAN JESUS. HE GOES BACK FOR THE REST IN THAT FIELD. HE KNOWS THERES MORE TREASURE AND IS NOT SATISFIED WITH JUST THAT TASTE OF SALVATION & JESUS. JESUS IS NOT JUST A *SIDE ORDER* TO HIM!!

3. HEBREWS 11:6 "...HE REWARDS THOSE WHO DILIGENTLY SEEK HIM". IF YOU AREN'T SERIOUSLY AND REGULARLY STUDYING YOUR BIBLE WHERE GOD CAN BE FOUND IN HIS WORD, THEN GOD IS JUST A *SIDE ORDER* IN YOUR LIFE. DILIGENTLY MEANS MORE THAN STUDY IN CHURCH, IT MEANS IN ON YOUR OWN TIME.

4. MATT. 7:13-14 "...FEW FIND LIFE...MANY GO INTO DESTRUCTION...". THIS TELLS IF YOU ARE SPIRITUALLY INTERPRETING SCRIPTURE, OR USING HUMAN WISDOM. THE MANY GOING TO DESTRUCTION ARE NOT SINNERS BUT CHRISTIANS. THAT'S HOW MANY CHRISTIANS WILL BE MISLEAD BY FALSE PREACHING & DENOMINATIONS. THE PROOF IS IN THE IS IN THE NEXT VERSE. *MATT. 13:15 "...BEWARE FALSE PROPHETS" THE UNSAVED AREN'T LISTENING TO ANY PREACHERS. CHRISTAINS ARE.*

5. MATT. 24:11 & 24 "...MANY FALSE PROPHETS SHALL COME AND DECEIVE MANY". MANY MEANS MOST. SO IF THE MAJORITY OF CHRICTIANS WILL BE TRICKED WHO CAN NOT BE TRICKED AT ALL? ***MATT. 24:24 "...IF IT WERE POSSIBLE THEY WOULD FOOL THE ELECT". THE ELECT ARE

TRUE DILIGENTLY SEKING CHRISTIANS WHO LIVE NOT FOR THEMSELVES. MATT. 7:20 "...YOU SHALL KNOW FALSE PROHETS BY THEIR FRUITS "[PREACHING & WORKS]. *SIDE ORDER CHRISTIANS CAN'T TELL GOOD FROM BAD FRUIT BECAUSE THEY DON'T DILIGENTLY SEEK GOD!!! CAN YOU NAME 100 FAKE PREACHERS ON T.V. & IN YOUR CITY; YOU JUST MAY BE FOLLOWING ONE; AND CHRIST IS ONLY A SIDE ORDER IN YOUR LIFE!!!*

6. 1 JOHN 2:15-17 "...LOVE NOT THE WORLD NOR THINGS IN THE WORLD...". IF NEW CARS, CLOTHES, ELECTRONIC DEVISES, FAME, WEALTH ETC. EXCITE YOU; THEN YOUR MIND & DESIRES ARE NOT FOCUSED ON SPIRITUAL THINGS. TO A TRUE CHRISTIAN A CAR IS JUST A CAR & CLOTHES JUST CLOTHES. WE DON'T CHASE THE DEVILS MATERIAL THINGS. OUR EXCITEMENT IS THE NEXT WORLD WITH JESUS.

7. PSALMS 1:2 "...HIS DELIGHT IS IN THE LAW OF THE LORD....IN THAT LAW HE MEDITATES DAY AND NIGHT...". THIS CHRISTIANS JOY & PLEASURE COMES FROM GODS WORD THE BIBLE. IF TOO MANY SCRIPTURES BORE YOU THERES SOMETHING WRONG WITH "YOU". NOTIICE HE THINKS ON THE THINGS OF GOD "DAY AND NIGHT". MOST SAY THIS PERSON IS A FANANTIC. SIDE ORDER & CASUAL CHRISTIANS THINK ON CHRIST ON SUNDAYS, AND WITNESS AND STUDY VERY SELDOM IF EVER.

8. MATT. 15:8-9 "...HONOR WITH LIPS BUT HEART IS FAR FROM ME.....IN VAIN THEY WORSHIP ME TEACHING FOR DOCTRINES THE COMMANDS

OF MEN". JESUS SAID "YOU WILL KNOW THEM BY THEIR FRUITS [TEACHING & WORKS]. BUT THE PROBLEM IS MOST CHRISTIANS DON'T KNOW GOOD FRUIT FROM BAD. SO THE WORSHIP MOST GIVE GOD IS A HUMAN TAUGHT WORSHIP & NOT WHAT HE WANTS. THEY FOLLOW THE "TRADITION OF THE ELDERS' BEFORE THEM. THEIR PREACHING IS DILUTED WITH HUMAN LAWS MIXED IN WITH GODS, MAKING IT ALL VOID. WHICH IS WHY JESUS SAYS; "IN VAIN THEY WORSHIP ME". THEY ARE CASUAL SIDE ORDER CHRISTIANS.

9. JOHN 15:8 "...HEREIN IS THE FATHER GLORIFIED THAT YOU BEAR MUCH FRUIT". WITH ALL YOUR SINGING & SHOUTING, & JUST ATTENDING CHURCH; "WITNESSING IS WHAT HE TRULY WANTS. " THE HARVEST IS PLENTIFUL, BUT THE LABORERS ARE FEW". JOHN 15:2 "...EVERY BRANCH IN ME THAT BEARS NOT FRUIT MY FATHER TAKES IT AWAY". NOT WITNESSING WILL GET YOU CAST OUT NO MATTER WHAT ELSE YOU TRY TO DO FOR HIM. REAL CHRISTIANS WITNESS; SIDE ORDERS CHRISTIANS DON'T!!!

10. MATT. 13:23 "...SEED ON GOOD GROUND UNDERSTANDS THE WORD AND BEARS FRUIT..". OF THE 4 SEEDS ONLY ONE UNDERSTOOD WHAT PLEASES GOD. HE UNDERSTOOD HE MUST WORK BY WITNESSING ABOUT GOD TO OTHERS. THE OTHERS SEEDS DIDN'T HAVE THE TIME OR FAITH OR TO DO IT. CASUAL, SIDE ORDER CHRISTIANS HAVE EVERYTHING ELSE ON THEIR AGENDA TO DO FIRST.

11. MATT. 11:29 "...LEARN FROM ME...". THIS IS THE KEY TO ABSOLUTE VICTORY AND HEAVEN. YOU CAN AND MUST GET YOUR TEACHING FROM THE SOURCE WHICH IS JESUS CHRIST THROUGH THE HOLY SPIRIT. YOU WILL NEVER GET TRICKED BY FALSE PREACHERS THIS WAY [MATT.24:24] STOP THINKING BIBLE COLLEGE, SEMINARY ETC ARE THE WAY. WHO EVER ATTANDS THESE SCHOOLS INSULTS TO THE HOLY GHOST!! CHECK THESE SCRIPTURES; 1 JOHN 2:27 "...YOU NEED NOT ANY MAN TEACH YOU.." GAL. 1:11-12 "...GOSPEL NOT FROM MAN...NOR TAUGHT BY MAN...". MATT. 16:17 '..FLESH & BLOOD HAS NOT REVEALED THIS TO YOU..". JOHN 10:27 "..MY SHEEP HEAR MY VOICE...". REAL CHRISTIANS LISTEN TO THE HOLY SPIRIT WHICH EXPOSES THE FALSEHOODS MIXED IN WITH TODAYS PREACHING.

12. JOHN 12:25 "...HE THAT HATES HIS LIFE IN THIS WORLD SHALL KEEP IT TO ETERNAL LIFE..". MARK 8:35 ".. WHOSOEVER WILL SAVE HIS LIFE SHALL LOSE IT". THIS IS THE FINAL TEST THAT WILL PROVE THE SIDE ORDER, CASUAL CHRISTIANS FROM THE TRUE ONES. REV. 13:15-18 SAYS WHO EVER DOESN'T GET THE MARK & WORSHIP THE IMAGE WILL BE KILLED ABSOLUTELY. IF YOUR FAITH ISN'T STRONG FROM MUCH STUDY YOU WILL LEAVE GOD AT THIS TIME;[2 THESS. 2:3]. BUT CHURCHES HAVE LIED AND SAID THE CHRISTIANS WILL BE GONE BY THIS TIME. HERES PROOF YOU WILL BE HERE; REV. 13:10 & 14:12 & 15:2 & 20:4 ALL SCRIPTURES SHOW CHRISTIANS ARE & WERE HERE WHEN

THE 2 BEASTS & DEVIL CAME!!! CASUAL SIDE ORDER CHRISTIANS WILL NOT BE ABLE TO ENDURE THIS TIME.

CHECK YOUR LIFE WITH THESE DOZEN SCRIPTURE POINTS. IF YOU IGNORE ALL THESE, YOU DON'T OBEY THE BIBLE ANYWAY. HAVE YOU MADE UP YOUR OWN MIND ABOUT WHAT GOD WILL ACCEPT INSTEAD OF WHAT THE BIBLE SAYS? THAT'S CALLED "SELF RIGHTEOUSNESS" AND WON'T WORK. ADMIT YOU HAVE BEEN "LUKEWARM-CASUAL & CHRIST WAS JUST A SIDE ORDER IN YOUR LIFE AND CHANGE WHILE THERES STILL TIME. ASK YOURSELF DO YOU DESERVE THE SAME REWARD AS THOSE WHO LIVED THEIR WHOLE LIFE FOR CHRIST, WHILE YOU LIVED FOR MATERIAL THINGS & FORTUNE & FUN? YOUR TIME WENT FOR YOU & YOURS. YOU WILL NOT GET THE SAME REWARD OF HEAVEN. LUKE 9:23 SAYS; "HE WHO COMES AFTER ME "MUST" FIRST DENY HIMSELF".

THAT'S WHY THERES A "NEW HEAVEN & NEW EARTH". EZEKIEL 9:4 SAYS ONLY THOSE WHO "..SIGH AND CRY AT THE WRONGS BEING DONE IN CHURCHES WILL BE SAVED". IF YOU THINK WHATS HAPPENING IS OK, THEN YOU AREN'Y EVEN IN THE RUNNING FOR SALVATION. THE NEW EARTH IS FOR THE SIDE ORDER, CASUAL, LUKEWARM CHRISTIANS. AND BEFROE YOU EVEN GET THAT YOU WILL BE CAST BACK BY JESUS TO THE WRATH OF GOD; HELL ON EARTH; SLAUGHTER OF ALL LEFT HERE. REV. 2:22 & 7:14; DAN. 7:25; & HEBS.

10:26-29 & MATT. 25:41 & ISAIAH 65:12. JESUS DIED FOR YOU TO GET HEAVEN. BUT IF YOU DON'T OBEY HIM YOU WILL NEVER ENTER HEAVEN REV.21:27. 2ND PLACE OR, 1ST PLACE? IT'S YOUR CHOICE!!!!!!

Most books especially Christian books must have Human references in the book to make it sound credible. My book only has Scripture references because as in the name Absolutely Wrong we know NO scholar will approve it. This is how far the Churches have gone off track. When human approval is accepted over Gods scriptures as proof of credibility. They have made themselves false rulers over Christ's Church just as the Pharisees did over the Law. And no one dared challenge them. The ones in Chapter 2 the Church of Ephesus are not afraid.

"CHAPTER 1"

A s I said I would only point out the main and controversial points of each Chapter. Here the first main point is WHY John is on this Island? We know all the other Apostles were martyred during the great persecution by Rome. It was mass round ups and killings and the Leaders of the Church were the biggest targets. So yes they got John also and for some reason instead of killing him he is sent to this Island to die. I have read that he was put in boiling oil but it had no effect. So he was sent to Patmos. It makes plenty sense that an event like that would scare the daylights out those superstitious people of that time.

So why did he not die at least by then? Remember Jesus and Peter had an exchange in St. John 21:15-23 about what John's job would be as compared to Peter's. Verse 23 there says; "then went this saying abroad among the brethren that that disciple should not DIE...". Yes I know the rest of it implies that's not exactly what Jesus told him. But that would be using human wisdom to think just because He did not say it **out right** we discard the whole thing. It was put there for a good reason and I will explain it more when we get to chapter 11 concerning the "2 Witnesses".

Let's look at this first vision John has. He sees 7 candlesticks and 7 stars in Jesus hand. They are said to represent the 7 Churches and the leaders of those Churches. This is very important to remember when we get to chapter 2 and the first Church.

We all can understand why John fell down as dead when he saw such a vision. It would scare the daylight's out of any of us, especially if we were alone out there on an island. I will not spend more time on this chapter because I want to get to the more controversial things in the following chapters.

"CHAPTER 2"

NOW we start with the 7 Churches. We will see Jesus starts of by saying "I know thy works". He will tell each one what they doing wrong and right. He always starts with the right. At the end of each chapter He says the good that happens IF they overcome & endure to the end. And interesting point to notice is how the situation gets progressively worse as the Churches go on. When I summarize at the end you will see the whole picture of the 7 Churches clearly.

"CHURCH OF EPHESUS": This Church gets more compliments than any other. Look what they are praised for. It is their boldness to go against even leaders of the churches and let the chips fall where they may. They cannot stand them who are evil. This means IN the churches, cause there is evil in the world. Look today how many Christians do the most horrible things, and it's all over the news. But even going against all this they are NOT tired or weary or even thinking of stopping for Christ's sake. Ezek. 9:4 tells of a group who; "sighed & cried at the abominations done". If Christians cannot see the abominations done today by Churches & Christians "their heart is FAR from Christ". It seems these forgot something being so wrapped up in opposing false teaching and fake sinning Christians. They have left their first love!! In verse 6 remember for later "they hate the deeds of the Nicolaitanes". The first thing a truly saved new believer wants to do is TELL others about salvation. So instead of winning souls they got side tracked. They are warned to go back to their first work ALSO. Look what He says he will do if they don't; "remove thy candlestick out of his place". Remember the candlestick IS the church. So the Church will be REMOVED from that particular leader. These are Christ's true leaders of the church. Not these denominational churches whose jobs are in the hands of bishops chosen by men & can be fired by men. None of these even count with Christ. The ones who get it right get the "tree of life" if they overcome. This is Heaven!!!!

"CHURCH OF SMYRNA": Jesus says they are in "poverty". This does not mean poor but rather lacking in number as compared to the false churches who claim Christianity. He mentions "those who SAY they are Jews but are NOT". Jews here means Christian. Scholars will say this is replacement theology but read Romans 2:28-29. All Christians are spiritual Jews; meaning Gods chosen or special people. Anyone who accepts Christ is NOW Gods chosen. Synagogue here means churches. I so wish people would see there's only one true church and it is a Spiritual body. Christians will have more persecution from false Christians than the devil himself. Now verse 10 says something very interesting most miss. "Fear none of the things they SHALL suffer". And the devil SHALL …" do many things to them. *When did the devil ever go on vacation, and why is he not doing these bad things right then? The Bible says he's always going about to "steal kill and destroy". This may sound crazy now till we get to that part BUT THE DEVIL IS NOT ON EARTH AT THIS TIME. [I TOLD YOU, YOU WOULD HEAR SOME THINGS HARD TO ACCEPT.] Hold* on till we get to that part. Notice they "SHALL" absolutely, positively have "TRIBULATION 10 [SYMBOLIC] DAYS. So if scholars say no tribulation for Christians how do they explain that? They say the church LEAVES here after chapter 3, but this is chapter 2! It ends with "not be hurt of the 2nd death". Again heaven if they overcome.

"CHURCH OF PERGAMOS": NOW you should start to see

the picture of the progressive worsening of the Churches situation. Satan's authority is now on earth, NOT satan himself. They are still holding fast for the most part and are praised for it. It mentions a man named "ANTI-PAS" who was martyred. Scholars think this is some guy from way back when. It's not. He represents the 2 Witnesses who are killed off in Rev. 11:7 [hang on you'll see]. Notice verse 14 & 15; where false teaching has started to slip Into the Churches. One the Nicolatanes; has also slipped in. Remember the first Church of EPHESUS VERSE 6 where Jesus said THEY hated those people. So how did they get in now along with the doctrine of Balaam? It's because Antipas has been killed. He was the big hero leader. Nothing could get pass him. I say it's ironic his name anti pass means you can't get any false teaching pass him. Just like the Apostles could not be fooled or scared off. Christians need to grow up fast & stop depending on their leaders all the time. Jesus wanted to stay longer with the 12 but God said No, come on home. They had to take it from there. The 2 Witnesses with all their power will not stay here long before they are killed off also.

At this time the first Beast is here. Rev. 13:1-10 speaks about him. It says "the Dragon gave him his power & his seat…".Why would the devil give someone his job when no one can do it better than him? It's because he can NOT be here to do it himself YET. Which is why the scripture says "where satan's seat, or power is, NOT he himself. We will see when satan gets back here in chapters 12-13.

"CHURCH OF THYATIRA": Notice this Church has more verses than all the others. It's because this is the **start** of the worse for the Church. This woman "Jezebel" represents the "False Prophet" of Rev. 13:11-18 with the power of miracles the first Beast did not have. Also when he comes in the DEVIL is NOW back on earth Rev. 12:9-12. [Hang in there]. Jesus; "I will cast her into a bed & they that commit ADULTERY with her into Great TRIB..". Scholars say this means a sick bed; NO. It means give her a place, [time] to teach her junk. It uses the word bed because that's where whores do their business & she was a whore, queen or not. This will not be a woman either. Notice it says "adultery" not fornication. Adultery means you are MARRIED & go outside the marriage. These are Christians spiritually married to Christ. Matt. 24:24 says they can NOT fool Christ's true believers. So this will farther expose the ½ stepping, lukewarm, fake Christians. Jesus says He will cast them "into GREAT Tribulation" showing Great Trib. Is a PUNNISHMENT!! Rev. 7:9, 14 tells of the Great crowd no man could count who came out of GREAT TRIB!! This is how many will get the gospel wrong. They are not in Heaven but on the New Earth [you'll see]. They have Palms in their hands not Harps like those of 15:2. There are no palm trees in the Holy City.

Verse 23; "...I [Jesus] will kill her children with death..". Does any church preach Jesus will kill anyone? NO!!! They stay off any hard subject to keep the offering plates & seats full. Jesus tells them to "hold fast" cause He knows exactly what we are going through. Verse 26 says they who make it will be rulers over the "Nations" [of the New Earth]. Yes that is what we will do while in Heaven for ever; rule over those who were saved but got fooled or sidetracked along the way like these who followed Jezebel OR any others even before this gets here. The parable of the Pounds in Luke 19 speaks of this. We are about to go into chapter 3, just remember from the 2nd Church "..satan SHALL.." do this and that to the Church. Now you see him DOING it. And this is just the REGULAR TRIBULATION NOT THE GREAT TRIB. WE WHO ENDURE THIS WILL BE SPARED THE GREAT TRIB. Christians who fail here MUST go into that one also & will definitely all die.

"CHAPTER 3"

"**C**HURCH OF SARDIS": A quick review of the 3rd & 4th Churches. The 3rd Church the Beast of Rev. 11:1-10 has started. In the 4th Church the False Prophet [called another beast] comes in & with him satan himself, Rev13:11-18. It starts by saying "…they have a name that they live and are dead". The scholars say they are a dead Church. WHY? The next verses show it's not. "…strengthen the things which remain & are ready to die…" [So they're not all dead]. Verse 3 is a point none seem to get. "…remember HOW thou hast received & HEARD…" . RECEIVED & HEARD from WHOM? Don't jump and say Jesus because that's common. Here it is speaking of specific people who are the "2 Witnesses" who were killed in the 3rd Churches time & happens in 11:7. All 7 of these Churches start at the 6th trumpet & end at the 7th trumpet. *1 Corin. 15:51-52 "..We shall be changed in a moment in the twinkling of an eye at the LAST trump". There are only 7 trumpets!! I not found thy works PERFECT before God..". Do you mean at a time this bad we are STILL expected to be perfect? YES! If it could not be done He would not ask it of us. Whoever says "no body's perfect" does not know that Gods perfect for US is not man's perfect. If we do all that the Bible says and put on the whole armor we WILL be "more than conquers".*

Sardis is told to hold fast for Christ KNOWS what we are going through down here and we are able to endure to the end. Verse 4: " …a FEW names EVEN in Sardis…[even at this most hard of times] ..who have NOT defiled their garments AT ALL….& THEY shall walk with me in white for they are worthy". Yes only a few [narrow is way that leads to life and FEW find it]. I capitalized EVEN to put emphasis on it for it's NOT some Church way back when but what WE will face as Jesus told us in 2:10 what SHALL come upon us. Verse 5: "....I will not BLOT OUT his name....". Have you ever heard a Preacher say your name can be BLOTTED OUT the Christ's book of life? NO they never say it & if they did they would not know how to explain it. In this book I will.

"CHURCH OF PHILADELPHIA"; Here we have the Rapture in the words; "..I have set before thee and OPEN door...". That means they ARE coming in!! Because; " no man can shut it..". We must stop there and pick up a completely different thought and situation with the words; "..for thou has little strength & has kept My word & not denied My name". It is so bad down here for true Christians [cause there is a false set of Christians 2:9 & 3:9] and with the last bit of power they have they've used it to stay faithful to Christ even as so, so many have fallen away because of this FIRST part of the Trib. Here are a few scriptures proving there are 2 Tribulations. Rev. 2:10; & 1 Corin. 3:13-15 calls them fires; Matt. 24:29-31. Scholars just assume we leave here before any of it, but can NOT show it anywhere.

Verse 9: "..I make them of the Synagogue [church] of satan [Christians following false teachings] who say they are Jews [Christians] but do LIE; make them come and worship at your feet and to KNOW I loved YOU" [not the false mislead ones because they think THEY are the ones right & loved]. *When does this event happen? Actually it will happen every year when those who miss heaven & make the New Earth Must come up to the HOLY CITY to worship but they can NOT come IN IT [Rev.21:27]. Rev.7:9 &14 tells of the great number with white robes & palms NOT HARPS like those in 15:2 on the Sea of glass. Zach. 14:16-19 tells of this event as the "Feast of Tabernacles". Lev.23:31-44 tells what they BRING to that celebration;*

PALM BRANCHES! Isaiah 60:14-15 tells of them coming to "worship our feet" & notice in both these Old Testament accounts it says "..THEY came against US & hated US..". You see these fooled Christians will first BELIEVE the beast & False Prophet until they make the Image & mark laws. By that time it's too late for them to make Heaven, for to make Heaven we MUST not fall for ANY of the 3 tricks. Worship [in their heart] of the 1st Beast comes in a year or more before the False Prophet even comes on the scene. Rev. 15:2 says we who make Heaven did NOT fall for even ONE of the devil's tricks. "worship of the BEAST or IMAGE or get his MARK'. I'm inserting 2 Studies I wrote years ago on this called "3 Strikes You're Out & EVEN ONE STRIKE" . Verse 10; "..I will keep thee from the HOUR OF TEMPTAION.." . NOW know the horrific choices people left here after the Rapture will face. They will remember what the 2 Witnesses said about "who burns forever & ever for real in the Lake of fire. It's in Rev. 14:9-11 & specifically says ONLY those who "..Worship Beast & Image & get the Mark".Rev.13:8 says ALL on earth except true Christians WILL worship Beast [in their heart thinking he's a good person even the mislead Christians. At the Rapture Bad Christians will be cast BACK to earth. Rev. 14:17-19; calls them the Vine of Earth. If any on earth now get the Mark or worship the Image they KNOW they will burn forever in Lake with devil & his angels. Remember if they don't do it they WILL be KILLED Rev.13:15. Oh how great a temptation to die right then at that minute or Get the mark and live a short time to the end when War of Armageddon takes place. At that time ALL humans still alive & not killed by the plagues of God's Wrath will die! Rev.19:19-21. This IS the great Temptation; live a short time more & burn forever, Or DIE right NOW!!! Talking about being between a rock and a HARD place!! All of those who did not accept Christ before this can & WILL absolutely go to the Lake of Fire anyway, but those cast back Christians do still have a chance at the New Earth.

"CHURCH OF LAODICEA: We all know this Church is to spit out. For a better understanding we want you to put Philadelphia & Laodicea TOGETHER. ONE is going IN, the other going OUT. What you have is;" The JUDGMENT SEAT OF CHRIST" Ro. 14:10 & Corin. 5:10-11, it's another subject they don't preach on cause they don't understand how it works. You will learn it just hold on. We are going to hit the main points of this one quick.

To be IN Christ is to be a Christian. To be spit out means He is rejecting them. So how does the "once saved always saved work"? They say; "you just get a LESS reward"? These are going to a fire [hell]. Doesn't sound like any reward to me & 1 Corin .3:14-15 shows the person in 14 getting a reward & the person in 15 getting none & he must go through ANOTHER FIRE EVEN TO BE SAVED. THAT'S the fire of the Great Trib. Christians were not appointed to [Ro.5:9 & 1 Thess. 1:10] IF they get the Gospel right. Next see why they are spit out. They are said to be LUKEWARM. Jesus didn't say they were not saved just casual; mediocre; average etc. When you hear some say "it don't take all that, or he's a fanatic etc", just know it is YOU who won't be spit out. Real Christian's sells ALL forsakes ALL Lives NOT for themself, but for the one who died for them & 2nd Corin 5:15.

They are rich in material thing's ONLY, not spiritual. They think they need nothing and will throw it in the face of the TRUE Christian's. But actually are blind, naked & miserable! Now look; they are being offered a chance even though they ARE GOING to this fire. "REPENT"; WHO I LOVE I REBUKE & CHASTEN" HEBREWS 12:6. YES they still have a chance but NOT to make Heaven but the New Earth. This IS why the book of life is open again at the 2nd Resurrection Rev. 20:12, 15. Yes there ARE some names in it that were rejected at the 1st Res. And they were ALL saved BEFORE the RAPTURE. These Are the tribulation Saint's cause NO one can be saved after the Rapture, [Rev.10:6] because there is no more faith involved. We are saved by Grace through FAITH. You can also see this event in Rev. 12:14, 17. In 14 the woman [Church] is taken away from earth & satan. In 17 the devil makes war remnant of her seed [cast back unworthy Saint's].

We STOP here because the rest is for all of us. Verse 20 -22 Jesus is saying to us all; "he stands at the door of our hearts [minds].. if any man [singular] will open He will come in to him [singular] & sup with him [singular] & he [singular] with ME". This is all about an INDIVIDUAL who can hear Christ's voice and not the voices of these false Preachers and Churches. He knows only a FEW will step away from the majority and follow Him, and be in the minority. Most will trust a scholar who got his teaching from a HUMAN school, NOT the Holy Spirit [1 John 2:20 & 27]. Man's school gives them the praise of MEN not God. "What is highly esteemed among men is an abomination to God..[Luke 16:15]. There is Pastor Worship today and just like the Pharisees of old they Love the attention & power & money. Plus, 90% will never admit they have been preaching wrong all these years. They would rather take their whole church to hell with them than to lose their income & praise from their flocks high jacked from Christ. Nicodemus said; "...we KNOW thou are a man sent from God..", yet they went against Jesus all His years till they killed Him. I tell people the biggest harassment and attacks on true Christians will come from the false Christians not the unsaved!

Remember Jesus said; "he who loves anyone more than Him is NOT worthy of Him". He said in Luke 12:51; "suppose ye that I am come to send peace on earth? I tell you NO but rather DIVISION;". If we stay in a denominational church because our families were in it for generations we have made our choice. Jesus is the true vine; so who are the "vines of the earth in Rev. 14:18?

At the end of EACH Church Jesus says this; ".. He that has an ear let HIM hear what the Spirit says to the Churches". Will you start today taking the time to learn how the Spirit leads and not the easy way of just putting your faith in these so called scholarly leaders? If they are wrong you will NOT be excused for following them. Matt. 15:14 "if the blind lead the blind BOTH fall...".

Now we have completed the 7 Churches and many will say this is crazy. So will you stop here or continue on the rest of the book? "Many false prophets will come and deceive many". Many mean's most. Most will be tricked. It's your eternal life on the line so choose carefully.

"CHAPTER 4"

This is a Vision Chapter. Remember in the introduction some Chapters are RE-views & some are PRE-views & some visions & some right where they happen. This is a vision only. A door is open in Heaven and John gets to go up and actually see the setting up there. Let's pay careful attention because you find out some more things that you did not know. Notice John sees ONLY one Throne and ONE sitting on it. Not 3 Thrones. He sees 24 seats with 24 Elders [ex-human]. There are NO other humans who have been taken up there YET no matter what they say at funerals or the verse that says; "absent from the body is to be present with the Lord". These 24 are the "first fruit's" 1 Corin. 15:23, they are 12 from the Old Testament and the 12 Apostles from the New. Matt. 19:28; "ye shall sit on 12 Thrones judging …". "Out of the Throne comes lightning, thunder & voices..". Remember this because we will see this again in Chapter 8 & it symbolizes Gods literal presents of His power.

Now we see there's a "Sea of Glass" before the Throne. NOTICE NO ONE IS ON IT!! IT'S important because when we get to Chapter 15 we will see that SAME Sea of Glass WITH Raptured Saint's ON it. So how can leaders say the Church or anyone else is up there NOW. We will see when & who gets there before us in Chapter 6. The four living creatures represent the strongest of God's creation on earth. Lion, bull, eagle and Man. They are not bored doing only their praise of God continually. We think in human terms and mind set. When you live in eternity there is no time or any of our natural boring thoughts.

I want to stress the "SEA OF GLASS" BECAUSE WE WILL SPEND MORE TIME ON IT WHEN WE GET TO 15:2. Also the 24 Elders are all from earth John saw. Don't let the scholars tell you those represent the whole Church & millions of believers. Christians must be judged first. Aren't you happy some these horrible professed Christians will not make it in? Judgment is like a court. Have you ever gone to court and everyone was found innocent?? Neither will it be so at Christ's Judgment Seat.

"CHAPTER 5"

Here we continue the vision in Heaven with a "Little Book" in the hand of the Father on the Throne. No one is found worthy to open or even look upon this Book. This book is sealed with 7 seals it's so, so important. Even John weeps because no one is worthy to open it. Then right in the midst [middle] of the Throne appears Jesus Christ. Why was there no mention of seeing him before in chapter 4? There are no 3 Thrones just one. And the Father and Son and Holy Spirit are there. "I and the Father are one". They are Spirits and can occupy the same space at the same time. Notice David is mentioned here. Yes our David the adulterer and murderer. Isn't God forgiveness great!

Notice verse 8 where the beasts and Elders "fall down before the LAMB...". If the J.H. Witnesses ever try to minimize Jesus to you again show them this verse. The Father has no problem with them doing it. We see them singing a New Song but it's not like the new song the 144,000 will sing. This song they tell what it is they say, not the Song of the 144,000 in 14:1-5. We'll get to that if you haven't given up already.

Notice verse 12; "worthy is Lamb TO RECEIVE power etc..". Didn't we figure He already received it when He rose and said; "… all power is given unto Me in Heaven and earth..". So how does this work? When God says something it's as good as gold it WILL happen, so we can say it when He says it. This same verse is in Chapter 12 so don't say I'm taking it out of context.

The main other thing I want you get from this chapter is the importance of the BOOK because when we get to the next chapter the books seals will start to be removed. Look at the seals as 7 locks. You cannot open this most important book till you remove the 7 locks. Then you can put the books plan of Gods work into action. We all know the scholars put so, so much emphasis on the seals in the next chapter than the book itself. This book will be mentioned for the last time in chapter 10 before its plan is fully completed. The person who gets this book by that time will finish showing the mysteries of it! And yes it's called a mystery by God. Some Pastors today try and make Rev. a friendly happy unfearful book as not to scare their flock. They did this also in the Old Testament when Gods Prophets said doom was coming. It is a joyful book for those who follow the leading of the Spirit and not humanly taught, self & human appointed denominational Church Leaders. All baptized believers have the Holy Spirit but very few take the time to find out how He leads us. It's easier to just listen to the man in the pulpit and never go through the trouble of studying seriously for ourselves.

Some think that when they got saved every thought that came to their mind after that was from the Holy Spirit. This is why there is some very crazy things being done and taught today.

"CHAPTER 6"

N ow we are starting with some very symbolic events, and it's no wonder people just start guessing at this point. I said at the beginning there about 5 thing's the lord has not revealed to me yet and ONE is in this chapter. Notice it does not say when Christ opens the 1st seal that it is the 1st. it says; "when He opened ONE of the seals..". This is significant because if you have a good reference Bible you'll see 8:1 refers to 6:1. Someone was revealed the connection. 8:1 is when the 7th seal is opened & we see NO event, except; "...there was silence about ½ an hour..". We will get to that. *I must reveal one thing NOW. Everything we see when the seals are opened does NOT happen when they're opened. They WILL happen when all the seals are off the BOOK & the 7 Trumpets start to blow, then Gods plan IN the book can go into effect. It has to do with the ½ hour silence of 8:1. Remember it's the BOOK that's most important not the seals. It's the Trumpets that announce the start of each event.*

The White Horse appears & He has a bow and a CROWN was given Him & He went forth conquering and TO conquer. Nowhere does it say He is ever defeated. And no one can give a crown but God Himself. So why scholars say this must be a false Christ is odd to me. I say it IS Jesus Christ and He is going forth in the power of His Father. [..till His enemies be made His footstool..] He needs no arrows.

The Red Horse appears & power is given him to take peace from the earth. The Power is from WHOM? It's from the one with the

Crown of course. This is one of the 5 things I don't have completely clear yet. God has His reasons for not showing me this yet. I can tell you what I **think** I see. Who has taken peace from the earth in this advanced age from the rich countries? What is this great sword or weapon they have that modern countries don't. Suicide Bombers!!! The world can no longer be at peace. I don't mind being wrong on this because I admit the 5-7 cloudy points out of the entire 22 chapters. I see these as the terrorist worldwide.

The Black Horse appears & has a pair of balances in his hand. Scales and balances are used to even out 2 sides to show a weight. Before you jump to the food part of this being food going sky high stick with the balances. This is the Peace Maker of 1 Thess. 5:3; "…when **they** say peace & safety; sudden destruction comes…". And Daniel 8:25; "….by peace shall destroy many…". This is the 1st beast of Rev. 13:1-10 [the 666 guy] "who can make war with him" Rev. 13:4. This is a false peace that will not last but will encourage those who don't even care about the Bible but want peace another way. Yes there will be food shortages but it comes later. Look at the last words in vs. 6; "..See thou hurt not the oil & the wine..". Hurt not sounds like peace, and should not be hard to see who the oil and wine represent on earth. Peace & safety mean the same thing. Peace here means **"prosperity"** wouldn't the world just love someone who bring back jobs & money!

The Pale Horse appears & his name is Death & "HELL FOLLOWED WITH HIM".[INSERTED A STUDY]. Power was given him over the 4th part of the earth…" The 4th part does not mean a specific region, it means the world's last time as in Daniel 2:40-43 & 7:7, 19 "4th Kingdom & 4th. All this beast does is killing!!! The main part is HELL FOLLOWING. Shortly after this beast gets here there comes in literal HELL!! This is the point none can see even though it's written plainly. They don't say it because they cannot explain it. I will give you the short version now. This IS the 2nd beast of Rev. 13:11-18 who is the False Prophet. When he comes in the literal devil comes BACK to earth after his 1,000 yrs. bound. [Hang in there we will get to that]. The Rapture happens shortly after they arrive [Rev.12:12-14] & make the Image and laws to worship it or die. After the Rapture NO one can be saved who was not saved before the Rapture. The scholars have people being saved during the Great Trib. They do not know who the tribulation Saints of Rev. 7:9, 14 are. They are the cast back Christians who were saved before the Rapture while there was still faith involved. Once the world sees the rapture there is no more faith needed so NO salvation for the unsaved period. They are just like the DEAD in the graves now that cannot be saved either & have nothing to look forward to but the Great White Throne Judgment and the Lake of Fire. Jesus spoke of "2" Hells [insert on 2 Hells]. The first is the rich man and Lazarus, who "DIED & WAS BURIED. THE OTHER IN MARK 9:43-45 have nothing to look forward to but the Great White Throne Judgment & the Lake of Fire. THE OTHER IN MARK 9:43-48 WHERE; "..Their worm dies not..". That person is still alive on earth!!! I will stop here. The insert has more scriptures on it.

The Fifth Seal is opened and we see; "under the alter the souls of them slain for their testimony.". They NOW start to speak; "How long will thou not judge & avenge our blood.." [Insert on Judge & Avenge our Blood]. This IS the 1st Resurrection of the saint's that died before. They are out of the graves and are given white robes. They have been raised to life and look what they are told to do while their up there. "Wait a little season till their fellow servants & brethren [US] that should be killed AS they were [in a tribulation] should be fulfilled". **Let's look closely again at 1Thess. 4:16; "… the dead in Christ shall rise FIRST..". THAT IS BEFORE WE WHICH ARE STILL ALIVE!!** THIS "IS" THAT EVENT. I will not overlook the rest of this verse that says; "So shall we ever be with the Lord" because some think that part can be used to rebut the cast back scriptures. Paul knows exactly who the WE are that will forever be with Him that go up. In 2 Thess. 1:5, 11 he speaks of being "counted WORTHY". They have one scripture the Bible has many showing the cast back.

THE SIXTH SEAL is opened & we see the "…sun becoming black..". This is the start of the "OUTER DARKNESS" Jesus spoke of. [Time for us to go] We see "…the stars fall from heaven AS a fig tree cast untimely figs..". Jesus spoke of BOTH these events in His last sermons of Matt. 24, Mk 13, & Luke 21. *What are these STARS that fall?* It is symbolic of what or who? Daniel gives us hint in Dan. 12:2-3; "WE shine as the brightness of the firmament & as the STARS forever". All Christians are symbolic stars and the lights of the world. These are those mislead, no fruit bearing, sin willfully, unloving Christians being CAST DOWN. Daniel 12:2; "many shall rise [not all, so we know it's the 1st Res.] some to everlasting life SOME to SHAME & everlasting contempt". Most at the 1st Res. will not make it and get their feelings hurt like those in Matt. 7:22 who did "wonderful works". The FIG tree are the 7 Churches that start in 6th trumpet and when it "begins" to sprout forth [Matt.24:32 & Mk. 4:29] the end comes. Christians will have to make up their minds quick about joining it.

"Heaven departed as a scroll when it is rolled together". YOU should know this one!! The parable of the 10 Virgins and the door to the wedding was "SHUT" Matt 25:10 & Is. 26:20. NO one else got in the wedding, nor will they at the wedding in Heaven. This is why those at the 2nd Res. will go to the New Earth, Not heaven. The rest of this chapter shows the utter panic when God pours out His 7 vials of wrath on this earth. Not just women and children but grown men scared to death!

"CHAPTER 7"

Here is another vision chapter that is very symbolic also. But I always tell people the answers are usually right there IN the words. This starts again saying; "after these things" [of chapter 6]. John sees four angels holding the four winds. What are these winds? [We will see IN the words] Another angel comes with a seal & tells the four; "hurt not the earth and sea till he has sealed Gods servants. Notice verse 4; "I heard the number of them". Those same words are used in 9:16 and have a connection to the 144,000. Now he seals 12,000 from each tribe.

Let's analyze the sealing first. Remember Romans 2:28-29; "....He is a Jew who is one inwardly & circumcision is that of the heart, IN spirit & not letter..". Everyone who accepts Jesus Christ IS a Spiritual Jew. God keeps that name as His Chosen people. If the Jews do not accept Christ they go the same hell & lake of Fire as everyone else. Who would let someone who rejected the death of their child FOR THEM still be special in their eyes? Jesus warned them to leave Jerusalem before the massacre in 70AD. He said; "When you the abomination of desolation.... Flee". This abomination happened in 67AD and Christ's true followers left. God knows where "those" who left are NOW. The ones there in 70 were those who did NOT heed Jesus warning. They were taken into captivity in Rome & in slaved & spread throughout Europe for 1,900 years, cross breeding with all. Those in Israel now still don't accept Jesus, but to the Old Testament. So will God pick 144,000 from there? Where are the ones who left in 67 AD? God knows where He places every believer in Christ. If He says there from a certain tribe then that's that! I will not dwell on race here, but read 2 Kings 5:27 if you want to.

The 4 Winds are the 1st 4 Trumpets of REV. that start blowing in chapter 8:7-12. Notice what the 4 DO. They HURT the earth and sea as 7:3 says. Now look at 8:13 speaking of the next 3 trumpets. "Woe, woe, woe to the inhibitors of the earth..". Now it's not the land & sea to be hurt but people. So the angels with the 4 winds are told **"do not hurt anything till we seal the 144,000". The 144,000 are here NOW** and just waiting on God to give the go ahead. All things are done on Gods time not when we want. I tell you **we are IN the 6th trumpet right now.** We will see the 144,000 2 more times in Chapter 9 & 14 and see what their job is.

7:9 we see the "Great multitude no man can count". These are BEFORE the Throne. The Throne is IN the Holy City. They are not IN the City but outside in front because they can NOT go In Rev21:27. They have palms in their hands. There are NO palm trees in the Holy City, so they cannot have gotten them from anywhere but the New Earth. This is Heavenly, Holy Jerusalem & City of gold. **There is another Jerusalem City on EARTH. You can read about it in Ezekiel Chapters 40-48.** It describes it in detail & is for those who missed Heaven. Check the measurements of that one to the Holy City in Rev. 21. Read Ezekiel 47 about the water that comes under a door and becomes a huge river & no one can enter that door. As you read you'll see THAT Jerusalem has not been built yet, but will be there after the 2nd Resurrection!

Let's check more in 7 about his great number with white robes. Verse 13 the angel asks "who are these John'. John says; "you know" cause John did not know!! **14; "...these are they that came out of GREAT tribulation & washed their robes...". Remember 2:22 where Jesus said those who follow false teaching would be "CAST into Great tribulation"!! This is how many got it wrong from mostly**

following false preachers, denominations etc. Notice they "washed their robes". How did their robes get dirty? Jesus doesn't give out dirty robes. *We all at salvation have a symbolic white robe. And we dirty them when we disobey Christ. Paul says he wants to present us; "without spot or wrinkle". And remember 3:4; ".. a few names even in Sardis which have not defile their garments [at all and they were still on the earth]. We have now a symbolic white robe. Are yours dirty & need washing?*

Verse 15; there's that word again BEFORE the Throne. "Serve Him day & night in His TEMPLE". There is NO Temple IN the Holy City!!! NONE!! Read Rev. 21:22; "I saw NO Temple therein". So how can they be in that City in a Temple if there is NO Temple in it??? They are from, and ON the new earth. Verse 16 tells us; "They shall hunger NO more or THIRST or HEAT will harm them anymore". These 3 things are 3 of the 7 plagues God will pour out on the earth after the Rapture; Rev 16:2-8. The food & water will be in control of the devil & beasts [what little there is] & they will not give it to those cast back Christians unless they get the mark. Remember ONLY those cast back Christians have even a chance for life again on the New Earth. The others will go to the Lake of Fire.

Verse 17; The Lamb is leading them ON EARTH not in that Holy City. Remember those of us who make Heaven will rule over the Earth also. The Living Waters are the ones that flow from under that door in the Temple ON the New Earth Ezekiel 47:1-7. Everything those waters touch springs life. "God shall wipe away all tears from their eyes". **This same verse is written in Rev. 21:4 right after the New Heaven & New Earth come IN. Who is this who is crying? It is a joyful thing to make Heaven. These crying ARE the only ones Jesus said WOULD be crying. Those cast into outer darkness where there will be "WEEPING & NASHING OF TEETH". I'd cry my eyes out to if I had spent 40-50 years thinking I was going to Heaven and got rejected, like those who did the "wonderful**

works" in Matt 7. I would really be crying if someone had TOLD me I was in the wrong and I said he was crazy, and it turned out to be true. I was warned and didn't listen to him. I listened to a man who went to a human school to learn Spiritual things. I went with the majority when Jesus warned me; "few there be that find life". Now I'm with that great multitude that missed Heaven.

So you have Chapter 7 and will you be in this Great Number who starved, and cried your eyes out? Isaiah 65:12-15 tells of this same group. You DO have the Holy Spirit, learn how He leads!!

"CHAPTER 8"

The first verse of this chapter has a mystery even the scholars don't try to interpret. At least the ones I've heard. They say it must mean Gods awesome power is about to come. Others just say they don't know. Let's look at it; "When he had opened the 7th seal," THERE WAS SILENCE IN HEAVEN ABOUT THE SPACE OF HALF AN HOUR". Before I give my meaning let me ask you something. If you ask me what is 7 + 7 and I say "I have NO idea at all; then you tell me 7 + 7 is 14, HOW CAN I TELL YOU THAT'S WRONG IF I HAD NO IDEA? I HAVE COVERED & SPOKEN ON MORE OF REV. THAT OTHERS WOULD NEVER TOUCH. THEY DON'T HAVE ENOUGH CONFIDENCE TO SPEAK ON IT. Romans 12:6 "Let us prophesy according to the proportion of FAITH". Only 5 times in Rev. will you hear me say "I THINK".

Ok let's deal with this verse. If you have a good reference Bible it will have a referral to 6:1. In 6:1 it says; "when He opened "1" of the seals", not the 1st seal. It refers to the 1st seal which is the white horse whose rider has a CROWN & He goes forth; "conquering and to conquer"; which is connected to the 7th seal. I say that IS Jesus Himself not the false Christ. Before I noticed the ref. I was already revealed the answer but the ref. confirmed it more. If you can take a moment to think on this before you read my answer it would be great & a blessing to you. See if the Holy Spirit In you will reveal it. ******
What do you think they were doing that ½ hour? And how does 6:1

connect to 8:1? Most don't even try and say "it doesn't say so leave it alone". I tell you each and everything is in here is FOR us to know eventually and the time is now. Here's a hint; something MUST to be done before Jesus Christ can take control on earth. What is it?

Remember Jesus said; "No man can enter into a strong man's house and spoil his goods except he FIRST bind the strong man". Who is the strong man on earth? Even after Jesus rose from the grave & said; "All power is given unto Me in Heaven & Earth" did He take control from satan right then? We see in the books after the Gospels Paul & the others speak of satan STILL being ruler of this world. And remember chapter 5; "worthy is He TO RECEIVE Power". So before Jesus can take control He MUST first BIND the devil. **THAT IS WHAT THEY ARE DOING IN THIS ½ HOUR!! 8:1 must take place before 6:1 can take place.** The trumpets are about to blow & NOW Gods plan in the Book can be put into action because ALL the seals are OFF & it can be opened. OH there's more! When we get to Chapter **9** the 5th trumpet the Bottomless pit is OPENED & things come OUT. Nothing is going "IN"; proving the 1,000 symbolic years of the devil being bound is OVER!! We will get much more on that in 20:1-3 & 7 & chapter 12 even.

Verse 2 we now see the 7 angels ready to blow the trumpets to announce Gods actions about to happen on the earth. What we **SAW IN THE SEALS & 7 CHURCHES IS GOING TO START HAPPENING. THEY DID NOT HAPPEN IN THOSE VESRES!!!** Now we see an angel gathering the prayers of the Saints from an altar to place upon a GOLDEN ALTER. THIS FIRST ALTAR REPRENSENTS THE EARTH, WHICH GOD CALLS, "HIS FOOTSTOOL". THE OTHER ALTER IS THE ONE **IN HEAVEN.** The prayers from US on earth about the madness in the world AND churches is going before God in a special way. That same angel gets fire from the Golden Altar, and cast it into the earth. And look what happens!! "There were voices, thundering and lightning and an earthquake", ON THE EARTH. I said in chapter 4 remember what signs are around the Throne of God showing His presence; "lightning, thunder & voices. Now it's [His] Power ON the earth. His power is always here but not like this. He can intervene any time He wants, but He has set a day for all the payback. **Here is the 3rd one I say IS cloudy to me & it's the 1st 4 trumpets.** But here's my take so far. Mingled with blood means the new & horrible diseases we have now from aids to flu's. The trees being burnt up & grass are these Christian Denominational Churches being rejected as to far out of Christ's doctrine. Many times humans are referred to as "grass". Jesus said on the Cross; "if they do these things in a green TREE"; showing Leaders as the trees. That's why the 7 real Churches [that are one] start again. When there's so, so much wrong you scrap the whole thing & start over. There's only one Church & it's a Spiritual Body anyway. When you JOIN a denomination you are pledged TO that Denomination; THEN, BY them; to Christ. You don't see it like that but Jesus DOES!! Can't you see that? If they are wrong YOU go to hell also. **You can go to any Church that is not way off track. But put NO faith in them. Which denomination do you say is right? Will God accept all with good hearts? If you get even 10 different denominations In Heaven you would have one of the biggest arguments IN Heaven! God is not having that. If you NEED human support there's something wrong with your spiritual connection. I need no human support. I'm overjoyed when I do find some who don't either. We don't just PICK a Church; we are it & are already IN one!! It's hard but we MUST go to some Church. Try to help who you can before they kick you out. I been run out of 5 in 15yrs. Jesus said about true Christians; "They will put you out the Churches".**

The next 3 trumpets concern the harming of the EARTH [7:3] **LIKE THE ANGEL SAID; "HURT NOT THE EARTH OR SEA TILL THEY HAVE SEALED THE 144,000". NOW** they are being harmed BUT only 1/3. **When we get to the Wrath in Chapter 16 it will be 100% water and food & climate damage! Things are already dying in the sea where most of the world's food comes from. The fresh water rivers are already polluted to the point few can be drank from straight. The sun's ozone is messed up. The whole world's eco system is beyond repair NOW. We will all die from it if God didn't have that saved for Himself to do.** All through the Old Testament God spoke of; <u>**"THAT DAY".**</u> Well that day is very near now. This world would destroy itself IF Jesus had NOT been in charge. There WOULD have been a nuclear war.

Do you say the devil MUST be here because of all the horrible sin & immorality? This world will be shocked to know WE are the experts at sin NOW. WE are perfect liars, thieves, murderers, and at adultery etc. We could teach the devil a few things about sin now. The devil introduced us to sin Now WE got the game and gone with it. When people say; "The devil made me do it" that's a LIE. The devil is not here, but he will be BACK with a vengeance Rev.12:12.

Verse 13 we see the next 3 trumpets & have to do with; HUMANS! Don't keep believing we will leave here before the 1st Trib. There are **2 Tribulations. We found worthy will escape the 2nd Great one. This is the "falling away" in 2 Thess. 2:3 & the "seed on stony ground" referring to these last days. The "house built on a rock"; "winds & flood & rain BEAT on that house". Christians would have gone into the Trib. UN prepared IF God didn't send someone to REBUKE & correct the humanly taught scholars who say you won't be here! You will know the whole ending before the end because God will NOT let the devil SNEAK anything in on Christians or those who would change, if someone had warned them. MOST will NOT turn from their Pastors& Denominational commitments. You'll see in chapter 9 only 10% of Christians living today will turn & be part of the 7 Churches & sprouting Fig Tree.**

"CHAPTER 9"

By now we know we are dealing with very symbolic words **that mean something else a lot of the time.** So here in chapter 9 verses 1-2 we see; "An angel ascend from heaven & opening the bottomless pit". The pit was locked why? We lock thing's to keep them in, or out. Nothing would voluntarily go, or stay in the pit. So it must have been to keep things IN, now they are coming out. We know only 2 sets of beings to have been put there. One set of angels in 2 Peter 2:4 & Jude 6; and that satan is said to be bound there a symbolic 1,000 years. That first set in Peter don't come out till the 2nd Resurrection. The devil & his angels are said to be put there the question is when. I say it happened in Rev. 8:1 during that ½ hour of silence. Now the pit is being opened for them to come out. **This is the event in Rev. 20:1-3 & 7. I tell people this is why scholars get it so wrong, they don't know what order this book is in. There are Chapters of RE-views & PRE-views. Chapter 20 IS a re-view chapter.**

Look what comes out the pit. Before it mentions the "locust", it spends time speaking of the "smoke" because we must first interpret the "smoke". Smoke is used for camouflage to hide something, like a "smoke screen" to sneak in! Now we come to the locust. We know NO insects are sent to the bottomless pit. So they represent something else; what? Why use the locust anyway & what is the hint? Locusts are known for many things but the first is GREAT NUMBERS, not their destructiveness. So we have a massive amount

29

of beings sneaking in under a smoke screen to do harm. Who does the enemy want to harm? Not the unsaved because he has them ALREADY in his pocket. It's the Christians he's after. What's the best way to disrupt believers trying to make heaven? Attack the head or leadership & get false teaching in to mislead the whole lot of them. And that's JUST what the devil's demons did. These demons went right to work & attached themselves to numerous Christian leaders which put false doctrine all through the churches. Jesus said; "Many false prophets would come and deceive MANY". Many; said by Jesus means an awful lot. LIKE the locust that come in great numbers. Look how easy it is to buy off, sex off, fame off, Christian Leaders. They were saved BUT when the money got right, & the woman was pretty enough, & the fame, & power over others got strong enough they switched sides. John 10 calls them; "hirelings" because they only preach for the money. If they had to live like the Apostles they would stop preaching. The Apostles had money laid at their feet & they KNEW BETTER THAN TO TAKE THAT MONEY & USE IT TO LIVE A LUXURIED LIFE! Not today!!!

They are deadly like scorpions not just a grasshopper. They are commanded; "Not to hurt the grass [real grass this time] or any green thing [proving they are not literal locust] but ONLY those men who have not the seal of God…". Get ready for another shock!! We know who are sealed, it's the 144,000. We KNOW the devil doesn't have to go get the unsaved because he has them already. So who does that leave? The 2 billion other professed Christians on earth [if you count the Catholics] who are not sealed [yet]. There is NO reason to go after the 144,000 anyway because they CAN NOT BE FOOLED OR TRICKED ANYWAY!! Matt. 24:24 "If it were possible they would fool the very ELECT". JOHN 10; "MY SHEEP HEAR MY VOICE" & "STRANGERS THEY WILL NOT FOLLOW". So they are after the people in the PEWS who don't have time to get serious with the Lord, and let the already demon attached Leader lead them to hell. [I know its strong language]. **"If the blind lead the blind both FALL". Remember the 1st Church of Ephesus Christians went AGAINST LEADERS & DIDN'T CARE ABOUT NOT BEING IN THE MAIN STREAM.** God does not give them permission to kill them [or they would] but to torment them a certain length of time.

Verse 6; "I THOSE DAYS SHALL MEN SEEK DEATH AND NOT FIND IT; DESIRE TO DIE BUT DEATH SHALL FLEE FROM THEM". This IS going to turn some heads!!! There has never been a time when a person could not die, that won't be until the Lake of Fire comes in. So what death is this? Jesus spoke of many believers "Drawing nigh with mouth & honoring with lips & heart [mind] FAR from His". The ones in Matt. 7 who; "Cast out devils & did wonderful works". ALL these thought they were shoe in's to heaven but got their feelings hurt. This death IS the death spoken of in Romans 6 & other places as "Dying with Christ to Salvation". Salvation IS dying to our old nature & it's all over the Bible but mostly in Romans 6-7. Think about it; with more False Preaching than true, how many are getting salvation that will last? Can a person even get truly saved from false doctrine? The devil knows he doesn't have to get you OUT of Church, just have you in one where you no idea what truth is from fake anyway. Jesus true followers KNOW His voice!! Remember the parable of the "Wheat & Tares"; the devil PUT people In Jesus field". Why? Not to hurt the wheat because the wheat can NOT be hurt by them. **IT IS TO MAKE <u>THEM THINK THEY ARE HEADED TO HEAVEN</u> WHEN HE <u>KNOWS</u> THEY WILL BE CAST BACK TO <u>HIM REV.14:18.</u> THE DEVIL <u>IS</u> THAT ANGEL WITH "POWER OVER FIRE" [AUTHORITY OVER GREAT TRIB. FIRE] WHO SAYS TO the ANGEL gathering the "Vine of the earth", to cast them BACK to earth; [send them back down here to ME]. He is laughing his tail off because he fooled the vast majority of Christians.**

And now he has a 2nd chance to stop them even getting even the New Earth if he can make them get the mark. [Take a break if this is getting too much for one sitting].

I'm going to move more quickly now. Notice the "Breastplates of IRON". In Rev 9:17 they have breastplates of FIRE. Which is stronger? Notice verse 11; "They have a king over them" whose name we know as the devil. Notice it does NOT say anything about what the "king" does. It's because that "king" is NOT down here with them yet. Yes he got out at the same time but did not have permission to come back to earth YET. So where is he? He went into heaven & we will pick him up in Chapter 12 as the Red Dragon & in 12:12 **he is cast back to earth for his very last time. [I told you would be shocked]. As we go along you will see it ALL joins together & makes sense.**

VERSE 12 & 6TH TRUMPET: IT'S ALL ABOUT TO HIT THE FAN "NOW". ALL OF CHAPTERS 2-3 & 11 & 13 COVER THIS 6TH TRUMPET. 14 & 17 ARE REVIEWS OF THE 6TH TRUMPET. "Loose the 4 angels in the river Euphrates". ANYTHING FROM THE EAST OR FROM THE EUPHRATES IS FROM GOD [REMEMBER THAT WHEN WE GET TO CHAPER 16]. These are prepared for "Hour, day, month & year to slay 3rd part of men". Let's start with the 4 different time frames. I will give you 2 scriptures. One is the Parable of the laborers Matt.16; "Jesus went out 4 times & hired & sent them IN the vineyard", [4 waves of crack troops]. #2 "The harvest is plentiful but the laborers are FEW; pray the lord of the harvest SEND laborers". So, so many THINK they are doing God's work RIGHT but they are not. They are working for a denomination or greedy Pastor who are reaping the benefits of their labor not Christ. To make heaven you must have it right!! So Christ MUST use ONLY those who DO have it right to fill the Father's House in Heaven. "In My Father's House are MANY mansions". The New Earth will have so many you can't count them all.

Now let's prove these ARE good guys. The set from the devil [locust] came in in the 5th trumpet. Does it make any sense to send in 2 sets of bad guys, From 2 different places? NO this 2nd set IS to counter act the bad set. These look nothing like them nor do the same thing. They did not come from the bottomless pit either!! **These ARE the 144,000.** Verse 16 speaks of another number; 200 million. How does this work? **It starts off with the 144,000 & from them & the 2 Witnesses 200 million of the 2 billion professed Christians today will come out of false teaching & traditions of their elders & follow Christ not a denomination!! 200 million is only 10% of 2 billion. The scholars say this is a 200 million man army that will march against Israel. Now do you see why there's only a few who find life. See how many the false Prophets fooled; 90%. See how many did not hear Jesus voice because they were so focused on their beloved pastors & the traditions they were raised in!! But look how many the 144,000 got saved? 200 million is a great accomplishment. All those 200 million saved will make heaven also with the 144,000 of Christians living today. Of course many from ages before will be there also. "And I heard the number of them", is the same wording used of the 144,000 & the 7th Day Adventist are the only ones I saw that made that connection. [All get some part right but are wrong on most ALL others].** Notice their "Breastplates" are of "fire". Fire beats the iron of the locust. "Out of their mouths come fire, smoke & brimstone". Remember this; nothing comes out anyone's mouth but WORDS. In 12 the devil is said to spew a "flood". The 2 Witnesses spew "fire" & Christ has a "sword". [You'll see]. The fire & brimstone means hard true preaching & not just a one sided thing of God's love.

Now for a controversial one again! "TO SLAY THE 3RD PART OF MEN". THE SCHOLARS SAY THIS MEANS A 1/3 OF THE WORLDS POPULATION WILL BE KILLED. **THAT IS HUMAN WISDOM.** The 2 Witnesses haven't even come in yet. Scholars say the 2 Witnesses don't come in till after the

Rapture. More human wisdom! If Christ came TODAY with all the confusion & false teaching less than 1% would make Heaven. Our God saw all this madness way back when. He took Elijah up 3,000 years ago for THIS time. Elijah is a killer prophet & yes God is sending a hit man with John. [We'll get to that soon]. **NO; a 1/3 of the world will NOT be killed then. What is man's first nature NOW? [TO SIN] WHAT IS HIS 2ND NATURE WHEN HE SINS? [COVER IT UP LIKE ADAM]. WHAT IS HIS 3RD NATURE WHEN HES CAUGHT? [_MAKE AN EXCUSE LIKE ADAM DID_]. WHAT THEY ARE KILLING OFF IS ANY MORE OF MANS EXCUSES FOR NOT BEING SAVED & GETTING THE GOSPEL RIGHT.** With all the false stuff out here Christians would swear up and down they had NO way of knowing the truth. But with the 144,000 & 2 Witnesses coming BEFORE Christ comes & giving them the truth they will have no more excuses. **Remember Jesus said in Matt. 24:14; "This" Gospel will be preached before He comes". Not the watered down, out of context, human wisdom, prosperity, race oriented kind, but the REAL Gospel. And God & Christ both have "sent one of their own IN the 2 Witnesses Rev. 22:6 & 16!!!!!**

Let's finish this Chapter up. Verse 20-21. Those NOT killed by these things did NOT repent. So that would mean NO one is left down here on earth BUT total sinners [if scholars are right]. Those who did repent and became truly saved are still down here at this point. There are STILL the 2 beasts & the devil to come. Plus the 7th trumpet hasn't blown yet. We don't leave here till the 7th & "last trumpet". You compare what the scholars say to this. At that time people can go back to being truly be saved, or Dying with Christ to their old life. Remember 9:6; "They sought death but could not find it". Now they can be from true doctrine.

"CHAPTER 10"

This is a short Chapter and is a Vision. We see an angel with the "little book" from chapter 5. This is Jesus Christ who actually took the book out of the Fathers hand. We see "7 thunders sounded and said something, but it doesn't say what. So we know that ONLY John knows the 7 thunders because he's told NOT to write that down [for us to see & guess at]. Jesus puts one foot on land & one foot on the sea & says; "...............There shall be time NO longer". This same verse is in Daniel 12:7 and symbolizes the 7th Trumpet. Let's see what He means; "Time No Longer". No time for what? It's not the total end of the world because the Rapture & Judgment Seat of Christ have not taken place yet. There are still people on the earth. So what is it too late for? 1 Corin. 15:51-52 says; "...We will be changed in a moment in the twinkling of an eye at the LAST trump". This event does not happen right here. I may have said before there is 7 places in Rev where the 1st Res. & Rapture are mentioned and this is what fools so many trying to interpret Rev. They think Rev. is supposed to go in order. This means; there's **NO MORE TIME TO BE SAVED FOR THOSE WHO DID NOT ACCEPT CHRIST BY THE TIME OF THE RAPTURE!** I said before we are saved by grace through FAITH. When the Rapture happens there no more faith involved. Forget these lying movies that show people getting saved DURING the Great Tribulation. It cannot happen. Forget what the scholars say about Tribulation Saint's. We saw who they will be in 2:22 & 7:9

35

& 14. They are Christians rejected at the Judgment Seat of Christ & cast BACK to the earth Rev. 14:17-19!

Verse 7 tells us that day does not happen right then. And it says; "The mystery of God will be finished" [known to all]. It will not have to be guessed at anymore. Look who it says WILL reveal these mysteries; "His servants the Prophets". **NOT SOME WHO WENT TO A SCHOOL & GOT A DEGREE! WE WILL SEE EXACTLY WHO THEY ARE. WE"LL SEE ONE AT THE END OF THIS CHAPTER.**

Verses 8-11 tell John to *"Take the book that is **OPENED** in the hand of the angel". Don't overlook "opened" because it's important!! When someone hands you a book you think you are to read the WHOLE book. But if they hand it to you OPENED to a certain place they are saying **"Take it from there"**. When John gets the book to Preach & do his part , more than half the book is already OVER by then. John gets it & does his part during the 6th Trumpet, and we are in it NOW! He will show up soon with the 144,000 helpers. There's NO time for them to be BORN and grow up, they are already HERE awaiting Gods timing & the go ahead. Now John is told to "Eat the book & it will be sweet in his mouth but bitter in his belly". Books contain information. So **all the information IN that BOOK is NOW in John's Spirit & only he can say for sure what it means. The 144,000 will ALSO be revealed some of this [we'll see]. Rev. may seem nice to some BUT the FULL knowledge of it is hard & bitter for the majority of the world.***

Look what John is told after HE EATS IT. **"THOU MUST PROPHESY AGAIN; BEFORE MANY PEOPLES, NATIONS, TONGUES & KINGS". JOHN DID NOT DO THAT BACK THEN HE WAS TOO OLD. HE STILL HAS THAT TO DO IN THIS TIME.** Writing the book for us to read is not the witness. I tell you there is NO record of JOHN dying. That's WHY he was on Patmos because the Romans couldn't kill him. I tell you he was taken up like Elijah [God doesn't have to tell us] & BOTH are here now. I said read JOHN 21:23 carefully. All Prophets were just normal people & different ages till God called them to work. The next chapter details those 2 Witnesses & there's MORE proof I'm right & not guessing like the scholars!

"CHAPTER 11"

THIS CHAPTER IS DETAILING THE 2 WITNESSES. We will add up the facts about who they are in light of scripture. We have 2 already. John ATE the book & JOHN was told he MUST preach AGAIN. Starting with verses 1-2 he is told; "Measure the Temple & Altar & them who worship **therein". This temple means the TRUE, fully dedicated with the right doctrine, Christians. He is seeing how many there are. Verse 2; "But the court that is without measure not for it is given to the Gentiles & they shall trample it 42 months".** There are 3 sets of people here. Those who are IN the Temple & Altar & those IN the court & the Gentiles. The ones in the courtyard are the ½ stepping, lukewarm, fair weather Christians, who WILL be cast back & the beasts & sinners will abuse them a length of time during the Great Trib. Picture the verse like this. IN Church we are on our best behavior. Outside in the [courtyard], patio, lounge area, parking lot etc. we can drink soda, snack. Use cell phones etc. Problem is these never go IN, they stay outside so they CAN do what they want. They think as long as they are AROUND & near the CHURCH they are just like the ones IN it on their best behavior. Look how many in Churches do NOT act Christian. These ARE them.

Verse 3 is God saying "He will give power [authority] to HIS 2 Witnesses & they will prophesy 1,260 days CLOTHED in sackcloth [humility]. How many of these highly educated scholars of today will submit to their authority??? Just like in Jesus time the Leadership did not submit to Him OR the 12, these today will NOT do it. The Pharisees didn't care who His Father was they would not let anyone come in & take over their rich & famous status. They would never admit they had the Word WRONG. And they will NOT do it this time either. I said they would rather take their whole Church to HELL with them first. Their ego cannot take a blow like that. Verse 4 calls the Witnesses what Zach called them; read it; in Zach. 4:12-14.

Verses 5-7 give the details of their work & the FIRST thing is; **"If any man will hurt them". Today anyone who goes against Governments, the rich & powerful, Islam, or even mess with the filthy rich Christian Preachers money by exposing them would be killed very quickly.** Look at the high profile killings of who those who spoke up for good. So God has that covered FIRST & says it first. But John is of another Spirit as Jesus told them when they asked to call down fire from Heaven like Elijah did. **<u>BUT ELIJAH WILL BE HERE WITH JOHN, & ELIJAH HAS NO PROBLEM KILLING AT ALL. HE'S GODS HIT MAN!! HE WAS TAKEN UP 3,000 YEARS AGO FOR THIS JOB TO TAKE ON THE SUPER BAD OF TODAY.</u> "Fire proceeds from their mouth & devours their enemies & they MUST in this manner be killed".** I said before nothing is coming out of anyone's mouth but WORDS. **It's whatever way THEY say you will die you will die that way & at that time. It must be done like this to discourage others from trying to kill them & proves they are from God.**

Verse 6 shows even more power they will have. **"Have power to shut heaven that it rain not [Elijah did that] power over waters to turn them to blood [Moses did that] & smite earth with ALL plagues as OFTEN as they WANT". Where's the Mr. nice guy Preacher everyone wants & likes?? Where's the LOVE Preaching?? Don't you have enough of them here already? No one's life is changing by their Preaching because when they sin** the Preacher just tells them; "No one's perfect & we all sin". Isaiah 30:10; "Speak SMOOTH thing's unto us" & "Teacher's having itchy ears". Yes Preachers are getting RICH telling the people what they want to hear, NOT ALL of what Gods book says. Acts 20:26-27; "I am free from the blood of all men for I failed not to declare ALL…".The seed on Stony Ground received the Word with JOY. But when Trib. came he fell away. Why? He was never **Told** about a Trib. He didn't expect a Trib. & he was not prepared, like the churches today aren't told they will go into the first Trib. He FELL, will you? These 2 Witnesses don't even have to & pray ASK permission to do these harmful things, they do; " **AS OFTEN AS THEY WANT**". WHY? If it takes a few 100 thousand to die to save millions, that's good a trade. **God Himself is going to kill off the entire population of the earth very soon after this anyway, so if killing helps save some, so be it.**

Verse 7 tells us **"When they finish; the beast that ascended from the bottomless pit kills them". No one could hurt them before they finished. This event happens in 13:7 & we'll see the 2 Witnesses come on the scene BEFORE even the first Beast to help Christians get ready for what's coming no matter what the scholars tell you. Why do they have to die anyway? Because they did NOT die before, and John is one of them. [If you want to jump the gun on John & Elijah study Rev. 22:6 &16].**

Verse 10 shows how HAPPY the world will be to them being killed. They will be so happy they will start a 2nd Christmas & give gifts to each other. Why? **"Because these 2 TORMENTED them that dwell on the earth". Even Christians think Preachers & God MUST speak a certain loving way & do certain things. Their heart & minds really ARE FAR from Christ.**

Verses 14-15 we see finally the **7th Trumpet.** This is the 3rd place showing the Rapture from Chapter 1 & there are 4 more before the end. No wonder it confuses the scholars. Now here comes the 3rd

WOE also. **"The kingdoms of this world are become the kingdoms of our lord** [See; "now" they are fully Christ's, not when He said; "All power is given unto Me"]. **Rev. 12:10 "Now is come salvation & strength & POWER of His Christ".** Why do Preachers say Christians leave here By Chapter 4? **Even this event does not happen here. It happens in Chapter 13. Actually Chapters 11 & ½ of 12 & 13 & ½ of 14 are one long event during the 6th & 7th Trumpets.**

Verses 18-19 is showing God's wrath getting ready to come on the earth. It does not show the details of Christ's Judgment here but will later. It does HINT to us that the Judgment took place because it says; **"Give rewards to Saint's who FEAR His name". Most will fear the beast's MORE than God and lose their life forever. "Fear not them that kill the body" like the beast can. Now He's going to "destroy them that destroy the earth". This earth was a paradise & sin destroyed it. Now all who have sin IN them will be destroyed. Notice the last part of verse 19; "Great hail". This shows the total end of human life on earth, because this IS the WAR OF ARMAGEDDON. Rev.16:21 will speak of this hail & so do scriptures in the Old Testament.** So if the 2 Witnesses kill a million or so it doesn't matter if it will make MORE see God is real and that accepting & obeying Christ is no joke.

"CHAPTER 12"

This is another very symbolic Chapter, but I have faith you will understand it. Verses 1-2 start with a "Woman clothed with the Sun, Moon, & Crown of 12 Stars". She is pregnant & in pain to be delivered". Scholars say this is Israel and the Woman is Jesus Christ, and the 12 Stars are the 12 tribes of Israel. That is the first thought that would come to mind "unless" we are not looking for a quickie answer. This is "too important to guess at". This is NOT Israel & the child is NOT Christ! Every time you see a Woman in Rev it represents a CHURCH. Chapter 17 speaks of the OTHER woman which is the False Church run by the False Prophet. This woman IS the Church & the 12 Stars are the 12 Apostles of it. [We'll see more evidence as we go]. Vs. 3; "There appears a Red Dragon" IN Heaven. Why does he appear here at this time & where did he come from? I said from chapter 9 when the bottomless Pit was opened and thing's came OUT, that the devil came out also *but was not permitted to go back to earth yet. We will see more proof in this chapter.* In verse 4; "His tail draws a 3rd of the Stars and cast them to earth". **Think hard now. The scholars say these are a 3rd of Gods angels joining satan!! <u>Why would a 3rd of Gods angels who SAW satan cast down & saw a 2nd set of angels of Jude 6 & 2 Peter 2:4 bound till Judgment; WHY would they now JOIN a losing cause with a loser they KNOW is very soon to be destroyed, WHY??</u>** Does that make even human sense, let alone Spiritual? It is NOT Gods angels being cast down. These are the same symbolic STARS in 6:13 & the same Stars Jesus

42

spoke of falling in Matt. 24:29 & Mk 13:25 & Dan. 8:10. These are the Saints that WILL BE cast back to earth. Daniel 12:3 hints to humans as STARS, & we are the referred to as Lights of the earth. **" The Dragon stands ready to devour the child as "soon" as it is Born"**. They say this was Christ & Herod having all the babies 2 & under killed was this event. Notice the dragon's MOST important focus is the child not the woman.

In verse 5; "She brings forth a man child to rule all nations & the child is caught up to God & Throne". They say again this is Jesus. In Rev. 2:26-27 who does Jesus say will "RULE WITH A ROD OF IRON"? WASN'T IT WE WHO OVERCAME? Don't they see we who make Heaven WILL rule over the Earth as Kings & Priests. In verse 6; the woman flees to a symbolic wilderness where" she has a PLACE [time] prepared, that **THEY should FEED her there 1,260 days". WHO is this that is feeding her?? It says it because we SHOULD KNOW who is feeding her OR it would not say it!! The person feeding her MUST have been mentioned in the verses before this one. There's a HINT; they feed her "1,260 days". Where do we know that number from? Rev. 11:3 the 2 Witnesses happen to be here that same length of time!!! And feed means strengthen & build up & nourish. _The CHILD is [are] the 2 Witnesses!_ You ask how can you get 2 from 1 person? If you can understand other places in the Bible that refer to the 2 Witnesses you will see they ARE sometimes mentioned as being ONE person. 2 Thess. 2:7 speaks of;** "He who now letteth [hold back] will let till "HE" be taken out the way [killed like the 2 Witnesses are]". The scholars put him as the HOLY SPIRIT, not the Witnesses. They say only the H. Spirit can hold back wickedness. Let's look at Acts 20:29 where Paul says; "I know that after "MY" departing grievous wolves SHALL come IN…". So it was Paul NOT just the H. Spirit holding BACK evil from the Church!!!! Remember I said the 2 Witnesses are HERE at the start of the 7 Churches in Rev. 2-3. Then when he [Antipas] is killed in 2:13 false doctrine come's BACK IN the Churches. Antipas is ONE & the HE in 2 Thess. 2:7 is ONE person. Why do we think we can put God in a box? Why do we think things must make human sense in a very **SYMBOLIC Book?** Remember when Elijah was taken up & Elisha asked a double portion of his spirit. "IF" he SAW him go Elijah said it would be granted to him. Now who did that make Elisha; Himself OR Both him & Elijah? Both the spirits of John & Elijah CAN BE put into ONE Body IF God wants it that way. And here the scholars are waiting to see 2 when only ONE may come. "MY GOD"!! How easy it is to confound the wise" 1Corin. 1:27. Verse 6 about the woman with the "Man child" is mentioned in Isaiah 66:7 and IS the same event & man child in Rev. 12:6. It adds something though. **"Before her pain came she was delivered of the man child". What in the world does this mean? The Woman here IS the Church also & it's saying; BEFORE THE WOMAN [CHURCH] GETS HER <u>REAL PAIN</u> OF THE 1ST TRIBULATION WHEN THE BEAST'S GET HERE; THIS CHILD [THE 2 WITNESSES] WILL COME TO STENGTHEN & SHOW HER HOW TO MAKE IT THROUGH THAT PERIOD.** That's what it means [take or leave it]. Because we KNOW & SEE none of the Leaders of today are even close to what is really coming on this world because Revelation was NOT given to them **for a REASON.**

Verses 7-9 we see the war in Heaven and the devil AND his angels are cast out of heaven. Verse 10; **"Now is come salvation, strength, kingdom & Power". As I said before it did not happen back then. The 7th Trumpet has sounded by now, & you saw this same verse in 11:15 where it says specifically the 7th Trumpet blew. Verse 11 proves the 1st Res, Saint's from the graves are up there from Rev. 6:9-11 & says; "They loved not their lives to the death". Verse 12 is the kicker! This is the Last of the 3 WOE'S.** "The devil is come down to you having Great wrath [anger] because he KNOWS he has but a short time". He will go to the "Lake of Fire" after this, NOT the "Bottomless Pit". **Verse 13; Please, FEEL the words here because if we know where to put emphasis on key words we will get the understanding. "When the dragon "SAW" he was cast into the earth...". Can you see how SURPRISED even HE was to be BACK on the earth? It's because he has NOT been here for a symbolic 1,000 years. He was bound & now his 1,000 years is up & he is going out to deceive as in Rev.20:1-3. Now he "Persecutes the WOMAN who brought forth the Man child". Why is he bothering her now when in verse 4 it was the CHILD that was the #1 target? WHY?** Because the child's job of feeding the woman that 1,260 days is finished & the 1st beast of Rev. 13 has killed him; 11:7 &13:7. The child is gone and the Church has been instructed by them how to endure these last days because NO ONE seems to be able to follow the leading of the Holy Spirit anymore.

Verse 14; the woman is given "2 wings of an eagle to fly away into the wilderness [different setting] into her place [where is a woman's place; with her HUSBAND Christ] where she is nourished for <u>A TIME, TIMES & ½ A TIME FROM THE FACE OF THE SERPENT"</u>. First let's look at "Away from the face of the serpent". This means the Woman is somewhere the devil can NOT see or harm her any more. Next let's look at the "Time, times &1/2 a time" that she's away. Please look at Daniel 7:25 where another set of SAINTS "IS GIVEN" to this evil for the EXACT "time, times & ½ a time". What is happening here? The ones in Daniel ARE the CAST BACK Saints from the Judgment seat of Christ found unworthy. This is all over the Bible, just not popular to Preach because it will make the offerings smaller!!

Verse 15; The devil cast a "flood out of his mouth after the woman to cause her to be carried away...". Remember I said nothing is coming out anyone's mouth but words. This is a flood of **LIES & not to literally carry away the woman because the woman is <u>already gone</u>**

<u>remember!!</u> The devils water or words can NOT reach Heaven. The LIES are for those on earth who now KNOW there is a GOD & has really raptured His people like the Bible & 2 Witnesses said. But they didn't believe it would happen. "But the earth swallowed up the flood", meaning they did NOT let that LIE stand because they KNOW what happened. Plus verse 17 shows WHY they knew. Because the devil is now; "Going to make war with the remnant of her seed". Jesus did not forget anyone. These are those Saints spoken of in 11:2, & Dan. 7:25 & Rev. 2:22-23 & 3:9 & 16 & 14:18-19 & Hebrews 10:26-29, need I go on. These are the cast back Christians who If while they are down here & don't get the mark or worship the image they can get the New Earth at the 2nd Resurrection. That's why the BOOK OF LIFE is OPEN AGAIN at the 2nd Res. Rev. 20:12-15. [I know that was a rough chapter & a lot to accept. My job is give it not force it down your throat]. Ezekiel 3:7 "They will not hear you, for they will NOT hear ME…………….". I pray you do!!

"CHAPTER 13"

This chapter has the details of the 2 beasts and is not as symbolic as most [to me that is]. As I said before the answers are in the words most of the time if we know where to look. This first beast is the guy with the so called 666. **Notice in verse 2**; the 3 animals that refer to his nature are "leopard, bear & lion". These are the first 3 beasts & kingdoms mentioned in Daniel 7. I won't show the comparisons but only one of those heads is alive & in charge at this time. The main thing we need to see here is the last part of this verse; "The dragon GAVE him his power & his seat". So before the devil gives this power this is an ORDINARY human. **Movies** show this guy being born a devil **which** is not true. Most of the world would sell their soul to the devil for power & riches like this anyway. Now WHY is the devil giving his job to this man when no one can do it better than him? **I said before it's because he can NOT be here right then to do it, but he will be back.**

Verses 3-4 show this beast gets "As it WERE a deadly wound & it was healed". Any time we the words "AS IT WERE" [we will see it again] we know it does not mean that literal thing. In this case the beast did not die & come back; he was very just badly wounded. It's such a miracle to everyone because yes he should have died not because of the wound but because of WHO gave him the wound!! Notice the end of verse 4 says; "Who is able to make war with HIM". Understand this picture. If he's so bad and no one can make war with him then WHO smote him despite all his power? Now you may believe what I said earlier that the 2 Witnesses are HERE also, and they are the ONLY ones on earth who has the power to smite him. now remember what is said about those 2. **"IF ANY MAN WILL HURT THEM…FIRE COMES AND DESTROYS HIS ENEMIES & THEY MUST IN THAT MANNER BE KILLED"**. All the 2 Witnesses said would die DID DIE but not this guy. **That's what makes his recovery so, so much of a miracle!! So we don't have to wonder who the beast is; he will be the one that DOESN'T DIE!!!**

Verses 5-7 show what he does after he gets healed. It did not say before what he was doing but he must have been taking care of his world business. But now look what his focus and anger is on, & who "He starts talking real mean, hateful, and vengeful"; but about who? Verse 6 tells us against the Saints and GOD and all who are in Heaven. Now you can believe it was the 2 Witnesses that smote him and now he's super mad with revenge on all who have anything to do with them. I know the Christians wish he would have left him alone, but this was Gods will & it's written. Verse 7 says "He makes war with Saints & overcomes them. The 2 Witnesses are killed in this also Rev.11:7. The 2 Witnesses get here a year or 2 BEFORE the 1st beast to help the Church prepare for this. Notice it uses the word SAINTS. Why because they are STILL here no matter they tell you.

Verses8-10 this has some super important information about who will make Heaven. "All that dwell on the earth SHALL worship the beast" [except] those whose names ARE in the Book of Life of the LAMB". Rev. 21:27 tells us "No one can enter the Holy City of gold unless their name is IN the LAMBS Book. If your name stays in the Lambs book you make Heaven. Remember from Rev. 3:4-5 Christ speaks of "BLOTTING OUT names from His book". All of the Christians who did not believe the 2 Witnesses will side with this beast BECAUSE they hate the Witnesses. Worship here does not mean bowing down, it only means think in their heart that he is some good and great person & idolizes him like people do movie stars. **Here is the important part; THIS IS WHAT I CALL "STRIKE ONE" [insert]. Rev. 14:9-11 tells us THE "ONLY" HUMANS THAT WILL BURN FOREVER IN THE LAKE OF FIRE ARE THOSE WHO DO 3 THINGS. #1 WORSHIP BEAST, #2 WORSHIP IMAGE, #3 GET MARK. All the rest from Adam will eventually get the "second death"!! So if they worship this first beast [and they WILL] they have one strike already. What's wrong with just one strike? Rev. 15:2 & 20:4 SAYS OF THOSE WHO MAKE HEAVEN THAT "THEY" DID NOT FALL FOR EVEN ONE OF THE 3 THINGS. SO IF CHRISTIANS DO EVEN ONE, THEY MISS HEAVEN. AND THIS THING COMES IN MORE THAN A YEAR BEFORE THE SECOND BEAST & MARK LAWS COME IN. When the 2nd beast comes in and makes the Image & mark laws THEN those mislead Christians WILL start to see they been led astray & fooled. But by then they will already have that strike one & can NOT make Heaven. They can still get the New Earth.** Verse 9 "If any man ears let HIM hear". These are the same words from 7 Churches. God knows most will not understand like many of you don't. But you must learn to know who God has chosen to tell you these truths. Is it the scholars or Denominations? Your life is at stake!! Verse 10 again we see the SAINTS are still down here. "He who leads into captivity will go into…". Means these false Preachers are have 90% Christians fooled & going into the Great Trib. [that's the captivity] they will go into it with you.

Verse 11-14: This is the beast the Preachers don't preach about & even Hollywood doesn't make movies about because they DON"T understand how he fits in. This 2nd beast is MORE powerful than the 1st beast. This guy can do miracles & the 666 guy could not. This guy is imitating Christ with his 2 symbolic horns LIKE a lamb". You see there is still religious worship in the world but ONLY that small few group of REAL Christians are being persecuted because they believed the 2 Witnesses & 144,000. The false Christians have had it easy & the beast is THEIR friend. But the devil doesn't want ANY worship at all to anyone other than HIM. Before I explain that let's look at what's obvious [to me], even though this guy is more powerful and does miracles he says don't worship ME; worship the other guy!!! When have you ever known a sinner to be so UN selfish?? Do you smell something fishy?

Verses 14-16 tell of the biggest deception ever to hit the Earth. And it will cause the most horrific of punishments the universe has for living beings [eternal torment with no death ever]. This 2nd beast will have people to make an Image [Idol] of the 1st beast. Then he will SEEMINGLY give LIFE to this IMAGE so convincingly all on the earth will believe it except those TRUE Christians who are STILL being persecuted. When the Bible says satan goes out to deceive the world in 12:9 & 19:20 & 20:3 it is speaking mainly of THIS event. What makes this so significant is **GOD SAID ALL OVER THE BIBLE THAT ONLY HE GIVES LIFE & IDOLS HAVE NO HEARING, SEEING, SPEAKING ETC. HABB. 2:18-19 IS ONE TO READ. NOW THIS 2ND BEAST SEEMS TO DO IT. This make him look like he IS Christ & God. This image starts speaking and giving orders. Once it starts speaking it is the IMAGE that running the world NOT the 1st or 2nd beast any more [Rev. 17:11]. This was the whole plan anyway. <u>The voice IN the image is the literal devil & he is a spirit and can do it.</u> It is the devil who gives the orders to *"Worship the image [him] or be killed". It is the devil saying; "get the mark". It is the devil whose saying if you don't you "can't buy or sell" [anything; even your own things].***

Look at the full impact of this. You can't sell your house or car or even get your OWN money out the bank unless you do those things. BUT you remember the Witnesses said if you do them you will "burn forever WITH the devil & his angels In the Lake of Fire"

Rev. 14:9-11. How will you feed yourself and your family? The True Christians are STILL down here also but we KNOW the timing to end from that POINT. How much will you lose in property & cash if you don't get the mark? You will remember Jesus said **"Lay NOT up treasure on earth" & "where your treasure is there will your heart be also". Christians have laid up & sought after riches JUST like the unsaved. They have big material possessions. They thought their heart was with & for Christ, but when this happens they find it really was with their money & property. They stand to lose too much to let it go. If they grab my bank account they will only get a few hundred dollars, so no big loss for me. Why when Christians read these scriptures they never ever dig deeper or just OBEY Jesus? "Lay not up treasure on earth".** What would it look like if the world ends and with all the poor & hungry & starving people in the world I HAD 20 MILLION stashed away for hard times? Now the world has ended & all that is gone to waste because money is now obsolete and all those people went hungry and died while I'm sitting on a fortune? How would Jesus judge me when HE told me not to lay up treasure on earth? And He was always helping the poor and hungry and I didn't?

"It is easier for a camel to go through the eye of a needle than for a rich man to enter into the kingdom of Heaven". There are scriptures that GIVE us a time line of the end. NOT THE DATE. 1Thess. 5:4 "But ye are not in darkness that, that day should take you unawares". The events of Rev. are on a timeline, but YOU didn't seem to be able to see it even after 20-50 years in Churches. You do NOT have to do anything but KNOW the TRUTH when you HEAR it! Jesus IS sending the truth about Revelation in Rev. 22:16. If you can't tell truth from err there's something wrong with your spiritual walk. "My sheep hear My voice". John 17:20 "Neither pray I for these alone, but THEM that BELIEVE at **THEIR** word".

Verse 18 tells of that now famous number 666. But doesn't say

666, it says; "six hundred threescore and six". Why not research that number as it's written IN the Bible. We can only use the Bible anyway to find the answer. It's funny what event that number refers to. But as I said we don't need to figure out who the beast is. **He will be the one who does NOT die!!**

"CHAPTER 14"

T his is a RE-view Chapter, and shows everything that happened from the 5th through the 7th Trumpets. This one gives the details of the Rapture and Judgment Seat of Christ. It does not call it by either name; that would make it to easy. If a Christian does not want to take the Spiritual time & prayer out to seek the truth they will never get it. We start with the vision of seeing the 144,000 and the voice of "harpers WITH harps". Harps always means they are going to or already IN Heaven. The big number with "palms" means they are going to, or are from the New Earth. There is NO Palm Tree in the Holy City.

"They sung <u>as it were a new song</u>". Remember what I said about the words "as it were", means it's not literally that thing. So this is not necessarily a SONG & not necessarily NEW. **And NO man could learn THAT song but the 144,000".** This means no man <u>could</u> <u>FULLY learn</u> it but them. Yes others can learn bits and pieces but not the whole song. So it's not NEW, it's been around a while, and it's not a SONG but a WRITTEN piece! I never knew what this song was nor did I even try to figure it out. Then one day while arguing the J. H. Witnesses one told me; "sing me that song". Then it came to me what the song was. The book of Rev. has been around and is not NEW, nor is it a SONG. And no one HAS learned it fully yet they Claim to because they have the Degrees. They feel they ARE qualified to SAY what it means. IF anyone can, THEY CAN, they think. And **what** UN educated person can say they are wrong. **The**

144,000 can and WILL & DO say they are wrong like the ones in the Church of Ephesus in Chapter 2. Now NO information is given to anyone from God without a specific purpose. It's not to just sit on. "He who has shall be given & he shall have more abundance [of info]". THE BOOK OF REV. "IS" THAT NEW SONG!!!

The job and use of this knowledge is to tell the Church in these last days. That's why no one could understand this book till NOW. Many wrote books with GUESSES AND MADE MILLIONS, BUT IT WAS NOT EVEN NEAR TRUE. "These were redeemed from the Earth Being the First Fruits". This means God approved "them" and their & works & heart, BEFORE the Trumpets even started to blow. That's why they were sealed in Chapter 7 BEFORE the Trumpets. Verse 4 proves it farther. "These are they who follow the Lamb wherever He goes". Not the billion Christians down here who SAY they do; THEM!! Phil. 2:21 Paul was looking for someone to send to Philippi and decided he could ONLY send Timothy because he said of all the Preachers he could send; "ALL SEEK THEIR OWN & NOT THE THING'S WHICH BE OF JESUS CHRIST". IF Paul said that about even Preachers BACK then, [before super hypocrisy came in] what would he say about these today???

"These are they which are NOT defiled with women". I said before any time you see the word "woman" it is referring to a Church, either the good one or the bad one. In this case it is the bad ones. These Churches here are the VINE OF THE EARTH THAT WILL BE CAST BACK IN REV. 14:18-19. THESE ARE "EARTHLY DENIMINATIONAL CHURCHES". IF YOU PICKED ONE YOU DID NOT PICK CHRIST AS YOUR NUMBER ONE SOURCE OF INFORMATION, OR LEADER. YOU FOLLOW CHRIST BY 2ND HAND INFORMATION. IF THEY'RE WRONG, YOU'RE WRONG. Why do you need a go-between anyway? Or is it you need the human support & to be in the crowd. Do numbers make you feel safe & right? Jesus said; "broad is the way that lead to destruction and MANY" are on that road. **These do NOT need human support. These KNOW the church is a Spiritual Body. These know having your name on a Church Roll down here means absolutely nothing to Christ. These have a job to GO AGAINST ALL this FALSE doctrine from ALL these women [Churches]. The 144,000 are spoken of in Daniel 11:33 & 35 also. These work WITH the 2 Witnesses, or the 2 would have NO help from the cowardly, human support needing, denominationally dedicated other Christians. That's why God only gives this info to them. No others can be trusted YET. Yet because BY their Preaching 200 MILLION will come out these; VINE OF THE EARTH CHURCHES and eliminate the middle man & trust Christ & MAKE HEAVEN. These know they will suffer MORE & longer than others before they get their reward. Do you want that??**

Verse 5 says; **"In their mouth was found NO guile [deceit]" . In other words they have NO ulterior motives, or hidden agendas.** These have no secret love of money and it shows by their lifestyle of what they wear & drive. They seek no fame, nor the desire to be a dictator over others like many Pastors. **"They are without fault before the Throne of God".** Why do people say No one's perfect? Why don't Christians see Gods perfect for HUMANS is NOT what humans hold as perfect for humans? All God requires to call us perfect is NOT to have any other desire in life but to do His will. He KNOWS we are imperfect & sinful & weak. So He only asks we be HONEST and Do what we say. What is a perfect Christian you ask? **He "sells all"; "forsakes all"; "lives not unto himself, but for the one who died for him"; "loves not his life unto the death".**

Now we saw the 144,000 that came in at the 5th Trumpet we move to 2 Witnesses, then proof of the Beast & False Prophet being here, THEN the Rapture. You will also now see **who burns forever & who does not. We were all taught you burn forever in Hell, but that's not true. All MUST come out of hell & we will get to that. Either we believe the Bible or stay in the traditions of our denominations.**

Verse 6 we see an angel with the "everlasting gospel" to preach to those on earth. I'm glad it uses the word "Preach" here so we will KNOW that NO literal angels do Preaching. It is someone else doing it. We KNOW who's preaching by the way it's worded; "To nation, kindred, tongue, and people". Where do we know that phrase from? Rev. 10:11 said that is JOHN who is to preach, and in almost the exact same words. Listen to part of the message; "fear God and keep His commandments". Why that when we all already know that? Because the beast & false prophet will be here and even Christians WILL be MORE afraid of them than God. "Fear not them that kill the body & after that has no more he can do: fear Him who **after he has killed has power to cast into hell; I tell you fear HIM". Even Christians fear death just like the unsaved. "Everyone wants to go to heaven but no one wants to die". "Flesh & blood can NOT inherit the Kingdom of God". The devil will pull out all the stops this time.** Most Christians will give in to keep from losing their money. If that doesn't get them he will bring in the death penalty on all who don't get the mark. **"He who seeks to save his life SHALL lose it". "They loved not their lives unto the death". Verse 8; "Babylon is fallen, is fallen for "she" made all to drink of the wine of "her" fornication". This Babylon IS the false Church run the false prophet. Rev. 17 will give the details of HER. Verse 5 says; "Upon her head a name; Babylon the Great"].** She is symbolically fallen because she has been <u>exposed</u> as a fake. This is the 7th Trumpet & the rapture will prove who was right, the little flock or that Great Number in the denominational Vine of the Earth ones.

Verses 9-11 show who <u>burns forever & who does not.</u> We were ALL taught we burn forever in hell, but that is wrong also. Rev. 20:13 "Hell gave <u>up the dead which were in it</u>". <u>These 3 scriptures are plainly written.</u> "If any man <u>worship the beast</u> [strike 1] <u>and his image</u> [strike 2] and <u>receive his mark</u> [strike 3] the SAME [person]. Then it goes on to say THOSE WILL burn forever. Why don't we accept that? <u>All others will receive the 2nd death eventually after they paid for all their sins. That's why the Lake of Fire is also called the *Second Death*"!!!</u> I'm going to leave that right there. Verse 12-13; we see again, like in 13:10 the Saints are still HERE. They have NOT been Raptured anywhere no matter what they tell you. "Blessed are the dead who die in the Lord from henceforth [that point on]". Why; because this is the time of the most killing of the Christians. This is 13:16-18 where the law comes out to worship & get marl or die. They're blessed because the 1st Resurrection has started & now ALL who die in Christ go <u>straight</u> to be with the Lord [no waiting] 1Corin. 15:22-23 & 1 Thess. 4:16-17. I know they tell us when we die NOW we straight up there because of the verse "Absent from the body is to be present with Lord". That is not for everyone except the 24 Elders who are the "first fruits". This is why when John went up there in chapter 4 all he saw was 24 ex humans. Paul & the other 11 did not fully understand either exactly how it worked, because that part was not needed back then. He did say "we shall not all SLEEP"; so he knew some would be in the graves till the resurrection. Daniel 11:34 is speaks of this time as; "helped with a little help".

Verses 14-16; we see Christ ready with a sickle to reap [rapture] the Christians. We see an angel come from the Temple in Heaven [proving Christ is not in heaven but in the AIR somewhere lower]. He gives Christ the go ahead to reap; why? "No man knows the day or hour but My Father". The Father sent word at the exact time He wanted it done. And in 16 "the earth is reaped". Reap means to bring IN. I say that because the next angel is going to CAST from UP there!!

Verses 17-20; we see "another angel he ALSO has a sickle". What is he coming to do? Did Christ forget anyone? No! Now we see another angel with power [authority] over fire. Who is this & what is he doing? He says to the angel [up in the air by Christ] thrust in thy sickle & gather the *CLUSTERS OF THE VINE OF THE EARTH*". THESE Clusters ARE the same BUNBLES of TARES in Matt. 13:30 about to be CAST & burned. Why group them together in specific groups? They are being put in the denominations of Churches they CHOSE on earth. They chose a "middle man" because they did not trust that they could make heaven or understand the Bible directly from the Holy Spirit they all had. This angel speaking from the "altar" [earth] IS the devil & yes he is an angel. He KNEW all along if those Christians believed his false stuff mixed in with Christ's truths they would NOT make heaven. This IS what ME, and the Bible & have been trying to tell you. Jesus said "My sheep hear My voice". Falling for false preaching will NOT be excused even though it does have SOME truth & good in it. Every lie the devil tells is wrapped up in some truth, but there's lies IN there that very few take the time to check for. Yes those mis-lead Christians are "fully ripe" for "trampling under foot" 11:2. **Let me add something of mine; the devil is laughing his tail off saying; "send them back down here to ME". His trick worked on 90% of believers. Yes 90% of those living in these last days will fall for it. Now he has a 2nd chance at them to get them get the Mark. And if they do they cannot even get the New Earth at the 2nd Res.**

The angel "trusts in his sickle & gathers the **Vine of the Earth & CASTS THEM [from up there] to the place where the wrath of God is to take place; ON THE EARTH!!** The sickle is used to symbolically make an opening between the spirit world & the phys-ical world, that's why it says "sharp sickle". Now remember each and every time Jesus said **"CAST HIM or THEM"**, no one ever thought where they are being cast FROM. They know they are being cast to hell but where from? Now we see where; from up there to the hell on earth for the living Rev. 6:8 which is the same living hell of Mark 9:43-48 "where their worm dies not & the fire is not quenched". **I know it's hard to accept this after you put your trust in other sources all these years. It's NOT Christ's fault. He warned of false preachers deceiving MANY. I also was raised in this stuff. Jesus hope is while we are In Him & in Church & supposedly studying our Bibles all these years, we <u>will</u> see that error and start following His Spirit. <u>Yes we all need to be taught at first when we are babes. But Paul says in Hebrews 5:12 most of you should be teachers by now WITH this right doctrine!</u>**

Let me say something about Denominations since I seem to hit them so hard. In times past I have known some VERY loving, witnessing, fully sincere Christians who wouldn't breathe unless the Bible said so. So what about them? This book of Revelation was not known to them like it is for us. They did their best with what they knew. It's so great what they knew was to reach out to get people to accept Jesus and live right. This is what the mission is anyway. **But none of those few EVER pushed the Denomination they were in; THEY PUSHED JUST CHRIST.** We push Christ, NEVER a denomination!! God is the Judge I know & He "winked at ignorance" once before. I don't believe He will hold something against a person who **<u>DID</u>** accept his son but had No way of even hearing this part to obey it.

Now; we today DO hear it & see there IS a Vine of the Earth. Jesus is the TRUE Vine so who are these Vines of the Earth? Revelation is being revealed in our time, so we have no excuse. So what can those who see it now do? We cannot UN sign the card we signed. The Pastors will not accept our saying we no longer want to be a member. All we have to do is repent in our hearts

& start telling anyone who asks us what the truth IS!! We can STILL go to that Church or any Church because we MUST go to a Church. There is no true Christian who says they have God in their heart and does not "go" to some Church!! Yes they will put us out sometimes & hate us a lot. They will talk about us bad & treat us like dung. It's been happening to me 15 & ½ years. Jesus said this would happen to US. But we GO and reach who we can. We don't disrupt the service or get forceful. We speak UP for truth when it comes up or in ear shot of us. That is our job. John 7:7; "The world cannot hate you but Me it hates, because I testify of it that the deeds thereof are EVIL". Speak up or lose out. Everyone who Believes & is baptized is saved. It's what we do & who we follow <u>after</u> we are saved that makes us go to Heaven or the New Earth. I CAN TESTIFY THAT THE "COMFORTER" REALLY WILL GIVE YOU SO MUCH COMFORT YOU WILL NOT NEED HUMAN SUPPORT ANYMORE! WHEN WE FIND OTHERS LIKE US WE REJOICE, BUT WE WILL NOT FIND VERY MANY. God is so loving & merciful; He put a clause in our contract [in a mystery] that IF we miss out on Heaven & being married to His Son we would get what I call honor roll mention or a 2nd place prize. Jesus only Preached Heaven because He wants us ALL to know we CAN make it. Why mention 2nd place & discourage some into thinking Heaven is to hard? "We are more than conquerors"!! It's our FAITH that must not be in anything at all but Jesus Christ. "My hope is built on nothing less than Jesus blood & righteousness* I dare not trust the sweetest frame but WHOLLY LEAN ON JESUS NAME* ON Christ the solid rock I stand ALL other ground IS sinking sand"!!

"CHAPTER 15"

T his chapter is a RE view & details of the Rapture that happened in chapter 14. We know this because in verse 1 John sees the 7 angels with the 7 "LAST PLAGUES" to pour out ON the earth. Romans 5:9 & 1 Thess. 1:10 tell us we are "saved from this wrath". This is what Salvation promises us that we will NOT be punished by God. But if we did not obey **Christ** rules since we were taken OUT from under the Law we WILL go through this **"chastening" as it says in Rev. 3:19. It is a whipping like a child gets, but they are not totally rejected forever. Only till this Great Tribulation is over like the ones in 7:9 & 14.**

Before the wrath is poured out we see "ON the Sea of Glass" Saints. Remember 4:6 when John first went up to Heaven he saw that SAME "Sea of Glass" BUT NO ONE WAS ON IT. The rapture did NOT happen there. The scholars tell us; "the church is not mentioned any more after chapter 3" so they ASSUME Christians left. Why don't they see that Saints & the Woman are mentioned & they are the Church? <u>Now look what they did to get there. They got the "victory over the beast, his image and his mark". I tell you again the Christians who do not believe the 2 Witnesses * 144,000 WILL fall for the 1st beast's deceitfulness & worship him Rev. 13:8; which will give them no more chance at Heaven. The New Earth is all they have to look forward to.</u>

They sing the song of Moses which is the victory song like when God overthrew the whole Egyptian army in the Red Sea. Verse 4 says;

"all nations SHALL come worship before HIM". That is those On the New Earth who MUST come to the **CITY OF GOLD THAT SITS HIGH ON A MOUNTIAN "ON" THE NEW EARTH"** each year to the worship & bring gifts. It will still be called "The Feast of Tabernacles" as they did under the Law according to Zach. 14:16. Then we see the Temple opened and the 7 angels come out WITH THE 7 LAST PLAGUES. CHAPTER 16 WILL GIVE THE DETAILS OF what it will do to those left on the earth.

Verse 8 says something very important. "No man could ENTER the Temple until the plagues were poured out". Why is this? Many places in the Old Testament God said "ye will SEE the destruction of the wicked". Isaiah 66:24 is one place. Rev 6:9-11 those raised from the dead Saints said; "How long doth thou not judge & avenge our blood on them that dwell on the earth". God said "Vengeance is Mine, I will repay". Many times in the Old Testament He spoke of "That Day". This IS that day & start of a period of time to repay ALL who sinned back to Adams time. I explain Hell like the county jail. It's bad but it's NOT where you do your time because you have NOT gone to court yet. When you go to court & the judge sends you to PRISON, that's when your time & punishment really starts. Court is the **2 Judgment Seats. One of Christ the other the Great White Throne of the Father. I ask people "have you ever gone to court and everyone was found not guilty? Neither will it be at these judgments.**

So after the plagues are poured out we DO enter the Temple. And what will do in there? Get married to Christ & have that Great Supper. And remember once we go IN the door to Heaven is **"SHUT". IS. 26:20; MATT. 25:10 & REV. 6:14 as Heaven being rolled together like a scroll.** Yes while we are having a Blessed time all those left on earth will be in total & extreme peril. Death, death, death on every turn Rev. 6:8. It is a literal HELL ON EARTH. Whoever does not die by devil or the 7 plagues WILL surely die in the War of Armageddon.

"CHAPTER 16"

This chapter gives some details of what will happen after Christians leave the earth. This is the day [time] God spoke about all the way back to the prophets. He calls it "THAT DAY". NO FLESH will survive this time. Anyone still alive by the 7th Vial of wrath will be killed at the War of Armageddon Rev. 19:21. In the very first vial we will see what I say is Gods compassion for man. Verse 2 shows a "noisome & grievous sore on they that have the mark of the beast & worship his image". I say compassion because remember 14:9-11 says is any human does the 3 things "they" will be tormented forever and ever. Notice it does not mention worshiping the 1st beast. It's because ALL will worship him except those whose names are written in the "LAMBS BOOK OF LIFE". BY THE TIME WE GET TO CHAPTER20 YOU WILL SEE THERE IS A DIFFERENCE IN "THE BOOK OF LIFE" & "THE LAMBS BOOK OF LIFE". So by this time only the 2 other violations [I call strikes] are left to be done. So God is first putting a visible physical sickness on those already with the 3 strikes to warn the rest of humanity NOT to do it. Only the devil & his angels were ever supposed to go into ETERNAL TORMENT "; NEVER HUMANS. But "they" that do the 3 things WILL suffer the same fate as them. People will remember that warning from the 2 Witnesses & most all will rather die early than get the mark and suffer forever.

2nd Vial is poured on the Sea & "every living soul died in the Sea".

Remember the 2nd Trumpet when it was only one third; well now it's 100%. Much of the world's population gets their food from the Sea. This is the start of mass starvation. Next the "rivers and fountains of [fresh] waters were turned to blood" [undrinkable]. Don't say it can't be dome all over the world. If God can do it in Egypt He can do it worldwide. Notice verse 6 shows why; "they shed the blood of Saints& Prophets & thou hast given them blood to drink". Jesus even spoke of the many killed by the time He got here. Then the great Roman persecution, then the one the 2 beasts will do to US before the Rapture [Rev. 6:11]. The next angel pours out his on the sun and it "scorched men with great heat". We already know about global warming, but this is something sent from God & much worse. Notice it doesn't say burned them up, just scorch to cause pain & misery. Yet men repented not. People will get so hardhearted they will never submit even in extreme misery & death.

Verse 10; the 5th Vial is put on the "Seat of the beast & his kingdom is full of darkness". This is their Capitol or governing body of leaders. It means with them having fooled the all those left here who TRUSTED IN "THEM"; and now they can do absolutely nothing to help them. The devil knew this all along but he & his angels **"deceived" the humans.** The human beast & false prophet and ALL they put in power around the world will see now they've been tricked. **SO WHAT CAN THEY DO NOW???**

Verse 12 tells us a mystery about Euphrates River. Remember I said remember anything coming from this river OR the East is good [good guys]. It does not tell us here, we are to search the scriptures for the proof. Let's go to DANIEL 11:36-45 which tells of this time & these same evil 3 in charge. Of course the devil is the real leader. This tells of the complete power they have over the whole earth. Then verse 44 says; **"But tidings out of the EAST shall trouble him".** The devil knows what and WHO is coming so he starts getting his armies together. Look who he gets? First we see "Three unclean spirits like frogs come out the mouth of these 3 & are spirits of devils working miracles". This EXTRA evil magic will help convince humans that they DO have a chance to defeat Jesus Christ when He comes back to fight the war. "They go forth to the Kings of the EARTH & WHOLE WORLD to gather them to the BATTLE of THAT great day of God Almighty". These are HUMANS the devil is tricking into thinking they can even beat GOD. The extra evil magic will make them think they DO really have a chance. I NEED you to go to Daniel 2:40-43. It's about this 4th Kingdom [last kingdom] on the earth. It's symbolized as "Feet & Toes; part of Iron & part of Miry Clay". Verse 43 say the "IRON will MINGLE with the SEED of MEN". We know the clay represents MAN, but what does the Iron represent? The scripture says "Partly strong & partly brittle or weaker". All angelic beings are much stronger than humans. This IS those evil spirits going forth the get humans to join them.

Verse 15 is just another warning to us because we are reading this before it happens. At the time of this NO one can be saved anyway so it's NOT to those still down here. Verse 16 they gather for this war. This War is mentioned 2 other times after this. Once in Rev. 19 when Christ comes back on the white horse **WITH THE SAINTS HE WAS JUST MARRIED TO IN HEAVEN FOLLOWING HIM [we won't have to do any fighting, He'll do it all}, the other in Rev. 20:8. This is why most get Rev. wrong because they don't the order its written in. it's not in sequence as it happens. It jumps around a lot & God only reveals it to who He pleases, NOT who wants it. Schools cannot get this right. God already had a set of people to give this to & THEY bring it to the world at His set time, not before.**

Verses 17-19 we see the very AIR is smitten. So not only are they starving, thirsty, sick and extremely hot, know they can't even breathe good. Now super earthquakes that never been heard of hit, and whatever is the Greatest city on earth at "that" time will be split apart.

Now Babylon the Great or the False Church; the Woman who rides the 7 headed beast [details of her in next chapter] will come before God for a **special and most fierce of His wrath & anger.** Remember these are ones who fooled those that DID at least accept Christ. And by them they are now down there dying with the sinners. This **IS THE FATE OF THE VINE OF THE EARTH in Rev. 14:17-19 being cast back to earth. This IS the Church of Laodicea** comprised of _tares, goats, lazy servants, sinned willfully, unloving, false prophet following, & fearful!!_

Verse 21 tells of **"HAIL".** This hail is mentioned in **11:19 proving again this book is not in sequence. The Rapture is mentioned 7 times itself. No human will survive this time. Those who feared death & the beast NOW WILL surly DIE. Jesus said; "he who will seek to save his life SHALL lose it". Fear will cause many to lose out. In Rev. 21:8 speaking of those who went to the Lake of Fire, before it mentions the murders, fornicators etc. it says; "THE FEARFUL". Paul told Timothy; "God has NOT given us the Spirit of Fear".**

This IS hell on earth for the living. When they die during this period they go to the hell for the dead TILL the 2nd Resurrection. Then they ALL MUST come out to be Judged Rev. 20:13. This is the time Jesus told us to _"cut off our hands & feet & pluck out our eyes rather than go to this place [time]._

"CHAPTER 17"

This is a RE view chapter of what happened to both the beast and the "GREAT WHORE" OR "WOMAN" OR "FALSE CHURCH & FALSE PROPHET". Remember I said any time a woman is mentioned in Rev it is a Church. There are only 2; one from Rev. 12 **"CLOTHED WITH THE SUN" & THIS ONE "DRUNKEN WITH THE BLOOD OF THE SAINTS".** She is a whore because a whore is NOT faithful to one, but spreads herself around and accepts all who come to her. It says **"the kings of the earth fornicated with her".** Meaning all earthly governments approved of her to be the only true & right Church ordained by God, when in fact their belief in her was brought on only the 2 beast's approval of her. It says "inhabitants of the earth were made drunken by the WINE [teachings] of her". Drunk; meaning confused & not able to see and act clearly like drunk people do. This IS also the "Church of Laodicea", and "those who SAY they are Jews and are NOT" Rev. 2:9 & 3:9. They are the "Vine of the Earth" Rev 14:18-19 who will be cast BACK down.

Now watch the way the angel describes the relationship between her and the beast. When we get through to verse 16 we will see the whole picture. Verse 4; notice the way she is dressed. She wears very attractive clothing fit for a high priced hooker. She's not your ordinary street walker. She's irresistible to most & she's rich. She has a name; **"MYSTERY BABYLON THE GREAT; MOTHER OF HARLOTS".** She is the center of & power behind

ALL false Religions or Vines of the earth. Jesus said in John 15:2 "I am the true Vine". Verse 6 says she's "drunken with the blood of the SAINTS & MARTYRS OF JESUS". WE MUST understand these are baptized Christian believers who truly accepted Christ BUT WERE caught up in false Teaching & Preaching like the ones who believed "Jezebel" in Rev. 2:20-23. Jesus said of them "They will be cast into great trib. & 23 Says; I WILL KILL HER CHILDREN WITH DEATH". This woman is the cause of ALL their deaths. Jesus said "Many false Preachers would come & deceive MANY" [most]. Why Christians don't double check their beliefs is beyond me. The angel is going to show John & US now how it will play out.

Verse 8 is long and will seem to be confusing, but we will break it down slowly. The beast "was and is not". Meaning <u>was here, but at the time of</u> *THIS INFORMATION IS KNOWN TO "US" HE IS "NOT" HERE,* "And shall ascend out of the bottomless pit". He will come back to earth later & be destroyed [eventually]. "And they that dwell ON the earth shall wonder [be amazed] at whose names were <u>"NOT WRITTEN</u> in the Book of Life". They will not be amazed at whose names WERE in the Book because they will KNOW who was in it because THE RAPTURE HAS TAKEN PLACE & THE GOOD ONES STAYED UP THERE. THESE WERE SENT BACK TO EARTH TO BE WITH THOSE SINNERS WHO NEVER ACEPTED CHRIST!!! We KNOW this because the last part of this says "when they behold [finally realize] the devil really is & who he is working through [the 2 beasts]. And when they SEE all the Preachers, Evangelists, Deacons etc. that they thought were so holy back here with them, they will be greatly amazed. In Daniel 12:2; "Some to everlasting life; some to shame & everlasting contempt". Daniel is speaking of the 1st resurrection because not ALL the dead are raised at that time. [I don't care what Webster says; in hells context everlasting means <u>as long as it lasts. That's why Rev. 20:13 shows everyone coming OUT of hell.</u>

Verses 9-11 is <u>so, so important. The wisdom spoken of here is NOT human wisdom & that's why scholars got it wrong.</u> "The 7 mountains are not the 7 hills of Rome, but the 7 continents of the earth that sit out of the oceans like big mountains. It means her false teachings & power are worldwide. Verse 10 says "there are 7 kings, 5 are fallen; one <u>"IS"</u> [AT THE TIME THIS IS REVEALED ON EARTH]; the other is NOT yet come; & when he comes he must continue a <u>"SHORT SPACE"</u>. There is only ONE head that can rule the beast at a time. The 5 fallen are the Great Powers who ruled the earth [run spiritually by the devil] in earths past history. Daniel tells of these in Daniel chapters 2, 7-8. And that's why this beast is described in Rev. 13:1-3 as being like a lion, bear & leopard which are same way Dan. described them in Dan. 7. Then he spoke a LOT about the "4ᵗʰ" beast & 4th kingdom & this is it. <u>The 6ᵗʰ king [head] is the beast of Rev. 13:1-10 [the 666 guy]. The 7ᵗʰ king is the 2ⁿᵈ beast 13:11-18 the "false prophet".</u> Now notice he's only in power a SHORT space or time. WHY because he quickly makes the "image" there comes an 8th king. <u>How do you 8 kings from just 7 heads on the beast???</u> It's because he is the one from the bottomless pit. He IS the literal devil. So how does he rule earth if he is a spirit? He <u>is the voice speaking inside the IMAGE that makes it seem like that Image is alive, Rev. 13:15-17.</u> He's not just of them he is the one pulling ALL the strings.

Verses 12-15 tell of the 10 horns [kings] that will GET power with this beast for an hour [short time]. They will of course not go against the beast, the one who gave them the power. **Verse 14 shows the "War of Armageddon" these kings of the earth get ready for the war WITH the devil & beasts.** <u>We know this because Rev. 16:13 told us of the 3 frogs that are spirits of devils GOING TO THE KINGS OF THE EARTH FOR THIS PURPOSE!</u> We see they have NO power against Christ Jesus & US who come with Him Rev 19:14. We are the ones in those "linen robes". There's more proof the great whore is worldwide & not just in Rome.

Verses 16-18 shows the most important thing I think Christians should know today. By the time these **turn on the Great Whore that was so buddy, buddy WITH the beast the Rapture is OVER. Now there is** <u>no need for her. Why; because the devil never wanted a church anyway.</u> **He only needed her to fool as many Christians** <u>as could so they would Not make heaven & would be cast BACK down here where he could have another chance to get them in the "lake of fire" if they worshiped the Image & got the Mark.</u> **Daniel also shows this in Daniel 11:37; "nor the desire of WOMEN" means the same as in Rev; women meaning churches!!! These beasts that used her & let her RIDE on their back will turn and kill her because GOD has put it in their heart to do it. NO ONE STAYS WITH A WHORE. WHEN THEY GET THEIR USE OUT OF HER THEY DUMP HER LIKE SHE HAS & HAD ABSOLUTELY NO MEANING TO THEM. And this IS what false Denominational Churches will be drawn into. They are not following all the teachings of Christ now. Over 100 Christian denominations divided by differences of teachings. Will Jesus excuse this? NO! Some do think the ones in them whose hearts are right will go to heaven. Can you imagine having 100 different faiths of people IN heaven? They would have one the biggest arguments in the world** <u>IN HEAVEN like they do down here. GOD is not having it.</u> **The reason this church is here is to distract people from the True Church and NO ONE WANTS TO DOUBLE CHECK!!!**

"CHAPTER 18"

This is another RE-view chapter. It reviews the Lords 2nd coming and the **6th time** the Rapture & first Resurrection has been mentioned in this book. The first was 3:8 **"I set before thee an open door".** The second was 6:9-11 **"And white robes were given to every one of them".** The third was 11:18 **"Give reward unto thy Prophets& Saints".** The fourth was 12:14 **"The woman was given 2 wings of an eagle to fly into wilderness, from face of the serpent".** The fifth was 14:16 **"The earth was reaped".** This is why most get Rev wrong. It's not in an order they can figure out with human wisdom.

Verses 1-5; shows things we have read already in previous chapters. A mighty angel comes down with the a glorious light and says; **"Babylon the Great is fallen, is fallen….".** We saw these same words in 14:8. We see there's nothing left down here but evil beings. It tells how many were made rich & enjoyed the prosperity of this wicked world government. Now in verse 4 we see the words **"Come OUT of her MY people & be not partakers of her plagues".** Showing God is about to pour out His 7 Vials of wrath on the earth. And we know Christians MUST leave before this happens, because **"We are not appointed unto wrath". So we see God has had enough and will now do what He said for thousands of years: punish all evil!!**

Verses 6-19 give us the details of all pain and misery and deaths those left on earth will go through. It speaks of fortunes lost. Businesses lost. Entertainment places closed down. Yes the parties are over ALL over the world. No more laughter or hope of any kind or for any pleasures ever coming back. They gambled and lost it all, even their very lives. I think all party people should read this chapter, but they don't even go to church. The rich & famous of this earth think the Party will never end and drinks will never stop flowing. They were blinded not just by the trick of satan but by their own greed & selfish self-centered ways. I said in chapter 9 about the **Locust that came out the bottomless & were told to only hurt them who had not Gods name in their foreheads. The devil already has sinners in his pocket. What he wants are those who DO go to Churches & do think about Salvation.** That's why he brings in a False Church & Doctrine and tells them **"they're all the same & serve the same God & nobody's perfect"**. The worst part is those mislead Christians will be down here **with** the sinners [**Heb. 10:26-29].** In verse 19 we see how fast all that can be and IS LOST, **"In one hour she is made desolate".**

Verses 20-24 we hear the angel tell those in Heaven to rejoice **"For God has avenged you on her".** This is the same thing the Saints asked when they were raised in **6:10-11 "How long does thou not judge & avenge our blood on them that dwell on the earth"? They are told rest a little season till their FELLOW brethren that should be killed AS they were; be fulfilled". I say all the time WE today will face the same thing Christians faced by the Romans [mass murder].** Verse 21 tells of a Great Millstone being cast down. This is most likely symbolic for the great HAIL spoken of 2 other times at the very end, even after the 7th vial has been poured out. Verses 22-23 repeat the end of ALL pleasures on earth. No more partying, night clubs, no more music to bring joy anywhere. It's because everyone now knows there nothing to be happy about any more. In verse 23 we see the words **Bridegroom & Bride being heard no more. This does not mean marriages, but the Bride being the Church & the Groom being Christ's voices ever preaching**

72

a salvation message again on earth. I said before no one can be saved after the Rapture. The tribulation Saints are those Saints cast BACK, & are getting the New Earth at the 2nd Res. Then it repeats how this false church & leader killed so, so many of Gods people. I have always said; "Real Christians greatest enemy will be the false Christians. Just the Religious Leaders of Jesus time that gave Him the most trouble & killed Him.

"CHAPTER 19"

In this chapter we will see what is happening in Heaven while the wrath of God is on the earth. We are up there having a Great Supper & Marriage and they are in torment. The door to heaven is shut so not even their prayers will help them now. In verses 1-5 we see **"much people" in Heaven.** So we know these are ex-humans. I call them ex's because we know **"flesh and blood cannot inherit heaven"; and we were "changed in a moment in the twinkling of an eye".** We see there is still a great focus on the **whore because that Church was our worst enemy. The sinners could care less about a Christian. And God is setting the worse on her.** Verse 5 reminds us again who we should really fear. *I use a scenario like this; if JOE tells me to steal BILLS TV, and I know if I don't do it JOE will beat me up. But if I do steal it BILL will kill me. I would be more afraid of BILL than JOE. The devil may beat us up, but God can kill us for real with no coming back. If we get killed by the devil God will give us our life right back.* Why people will the beast more is beyond me. Jesus said; **"He who will seek to save his life SHALL lose it".**

Verses 6-9 tell us "great multitude" which is combined of all from all the ages that made it be married to Christ. That sounds like a lot, but is MUCH less than the number who MISSED OUT in Rev. 7:9. A number so big no one could even count them all, who got the New Earth. We are about to be married to Christ & we get not just white robes but ours are **"LINEN". There's something special about linen that means RIGHTOUSNESS up there.** Now see it says we are BLESSED. The word blessed is used in many places & means they make Heaven. Daniel 12:12 "Blessed he that waits and comes to the 1,335 days" [I would love explain that one but not now]. Rev 20:6 "Blessed & Holy is he that has PART in the first res." Again those made heaven. Many will be called up but few will stay and have a PART in it.

Verse 10 has a sister 22:8-9 and is so, so important. John falls down to worship the angel that showed him all these things. Can you imagine how over whelmed John was by ALL he saw? He just had to do something. He had to show some sort of gratitude & that he was humbled. BUT he picked the wrong one to worship. That angel was very offended at him for falling down to him. Then In Rev 22:8-9 this happens again!! This is not an accident. It is a warning to US & especially Leaders of the Churches. <u>NEVER LET ANYONE GIVE YOU PRAISE THAT SHOULD GO TO GOD!!</u> Now look how much Pastor worship there "is" out here today. These Pastors love it, & some crave it. They are stealing Gods glory. Some crave "The praise of men more than the praise of God" Jesus said. When John gets back here HE will have people so over whelmed by HIM they will fall down to him also. But he will remember those 2 times and NOT let it happen. These 2 places are not here by accident. It's for John and US!!!

Verses 11-18 tells us something the Preachers never Preach about. It's Jesus coming BACK after the Rapture from Heaven, and not for any 1,000 year reign. **If heaven is "opened" it means it "must" have been "closed". That was the "Door being shut". He is coming in war mode to kill ALL who are still left alive on earth. Remember the 7 plagues killed most of them by now anyway. Churches never tell this side of Jesus. They only tell of His love and mercy and grace.** They forgot He said; "I and My Father are ONE". The grace period was over at the Rapture. I said many times NO one can be saved after the Rapture. The Tribulation Saints are those who DID except Him before the Rapture. Even they will be killed in this war. Rev. 2:23 "I will kill her children with death". Yes this is Jesus saying He will kill "all" His who fell for false teachings & preaching.

We will only hit on the main points of these verses like 14 where the "Armies of heaven followed Him wearing **LINEN!** We know these are the Saints who were married to Him because that's what they were granted to wear. He comes back ONCE for us, and again WITH US! Verse 15 shows He is in pure war mode. Why Christians don't speak of this side of Christ is a wonder. 2 Corinthians 5:11 says "Knowing therefore the TERROR of the Lord". But they still say the bad Christians will just get a less reward. What book are they reading? The slaughter will be so great an angel tells all the birds to get ready for the biggest feast ever. They will eat on the corpses of these so called super bad sinners. Several times the phrase "Free and bound" is mentioned when it comes to this slaughter. We need to reach out to those IN prisons also. I do.

Verse 19 we see the same thing chapter 16 says about 3 frogs [evil spirits] going to the kings of the earth to get them to join the beasts and devil in this war. I also referred it to Daniel 2:41-43. This is the famous **"War of Armageddon", spoken of in 16 and will be mentioned again in chapter 20. But in 20 scholars can't connect that one with these 2 because it would mess up their theory that the 1,000 year reign on earth takes place in 20. There is NO 1,000 year reign ON EARTH!! We will do the details of that in the next chapter.**

Verse 20 we see the beast and false prophet are taken ALIVE and cast ALIVE into the" Lake of Fire". Before the war even starts Jesus will snatch both of these leaders right out from their armies. Can you imagine what the others will feel when their LEADERS are taken without a fight. What confidence will they have then that they can win?? They came because he said they could win. And those 2 depended on the devil and evil spirits doing their magic. It was magic to humans but to God it was nothing. No power anywhere stands any chance at all. Yes the devil fooled all mankind who didn't take the time to seek the truth about Jesus Christ. They let others do their research for them about their OWN eternal life.

Verse 21says; **"The remnant was slain".** So after the beasts are killed **"ALL left alive are then killed". All, all, all!! Isaiah 65:12 tells of this event like this; "I will appoint you to the SWORD & you will ALL bow down to the Slaughter".** No wonder God asked in Isaiah 6:8 **"Who shall I send & who will go for US"** [to tell the **world the truth]. If Preachers today preached this their offerings would drop and most would leave the church. So they decided NOT to tell the truth, but make that money. And many others just DO NOT see Jesus doing this. WHY; because they are NOT in tune with the Holy Spirit to understand the Word. Or as I said before the things of the last days was never for them to interpret in the first place. God gives jobs; they can't go to some school then come in Gods house and PICK a job.**

"CHAPTER 20"

This chapter is a review of everything from the removal of the 7th Seal to 2nd Resurrection. The first 7 verses of this chapter the word 1.000 years is mentioned 6 times. Three concern the devil being bound and 3 concerns the 1,000 year reign of Christ. It is no wonder it confused so many scholars and others. We will break this down and find where people made their mistake. We will also see the War of Armageddon again. *Then we will get to the 2nd Resurrection and see **all in hell MUST come out!*** The Lake of Fire is now open for business for the first time also.

Verses 1-3 shows a "**Mighty angel coming down to bind satan 1,000 years**". We see in verse 3 he's put in the bottomless pit. And a "**SEAL is set upon him**". Let's understand what we read so far. We know Jesus said in 1:18 HE has the keys. We know a Seal is set over him. where does the Seal come from? **I tell you it is what they used that 7th Seal for that came off the Little Book. Remember nothing happened when they took off the 7th Seal, but "There was silence in Heaven about the space of half an hour".** I said back then that before the little book that was in God's hands could be put into effect on earth something HAD to be done. Jesus said "No one can enter a strong man's house & spoil his goods except he FIRST bind the strong man". This is satan who was always said the ruler of this world & Prince of the Power of the air being taken out of the way. Even after Jesus rose and said "**All power is given unto Me in heaven and earth**". The Apostles still kept saying the devil ruled.

The last part of verse 3 says **"He should deceive the nations no more till the 1,000 years were complete"**. The word deceive is key here because if you have a reference Bible you'll see it has referral to 12:9-[12]. That is when the devil is kicked out of heaven for the last time and goes out to DECEIVE the nations for the last time. **"After that he must be loosed a "LITTLE SEASON"**. We doing word connections here. Remember 6:11 where the 1st Resurrection Saints [not Rapture] are told; "rest for LITTLE season". Do you see all the times Rev says "short space" & "short time". This is that little season but it HAPPENED back in 12 not way back here in 20. You see in 3 verses it shows him bound & released after 1,000 years. It's because it's a **Review. The devil got out the pit in 9:1 when they "Opened the pit", but the devil was not allowed back on earth yet. That's why he appears in heaven in 12:3 but comes back to earth in 12:9-12.**

Now for another 1,000 years this time of Christ's reign with His Saints. Nowhere does it say that reign is ON the earth; nowhere cause it's not!! Verse 20 shows the "Judgment Seat of Christ" in some detail. Notice he sees **thrones [more than one]. And judgment is given unto them [more than one]. It is so annoying when I hear people say "nobody can judge me but God". Jesus is granting to His elect to do the judging as He told His disciples in "Ye shall sit on 12 thrones judging". And Matt.12:41-42 where He said the "men of Nineveh & the Queen of the South will condemn"**. And guess what else; these judging will not give a pass to their **blood** relatives. They have proved by their life they do NOT "love mother, Father etc more than Christ". **If just "1" sinner got on the New Earth after a short while people would have lock their doors again cause someone has started stealing etc. These on the thrones went through horrible things for Christ's sake. And here you have Christian coming to get in heaven that never did anything. When it rained they skipped Church.** _"And THEY lived and reigned with Christ 1,000 years"._ _So when does the 1,000 year reign start? Right after the_

"1ˢᵗ" resurrection, which is <u>before</u> the 2ⁿᵈ resurrection? Remember the New earth doesn't even come in till the 2ⁿᵈ resurrection!! So who says the 1,000 years happens on earth? This 1,000 years is symbolic also & actually is about 10 ½ to 18 months; or "time, times & ½ a time". If you compare Rev 12:14 to Daniel *7:25 you'll see "2" sets of Saints. One is "given" to the devil; & one" taken" from him for that" SAME" length of time.*

Verse 5-7 tell of **"The rest of the dead lived not till the 1,000 years were finished".** These are sinners who never accepted Christ who stay in the graves. Remember ONLY Christians get up at the 1ˢᵗ Resurrection. At the 2ⁿᵈ Res. All come out the graves because all will be dead who did not make Heaven. Verse 6 repeats that those "[accepted] has part in the 1ˢᵗ Res lived & reigned with Christ 1,000 years. This is the 6ᵗʰ time the word 1,000 years has been mentioned. Are you placing them to the right events this time? Verse 7 is very important and is the key to understanding this. **"And when the 1,000 years are expired [whose 1,000 years] satan shall be loosed out his prison". The order its written makes it LOOK LIKE it's speaking of Jesus 1,000 year reign. But it's absolutely not. Remember 12:12 is when the devil comes back to earth & it's just before the Rapture. If add verse 4 to the end of 1-3 you will see it lines up perfectly with the rest of the Bible on the last days.**

<u>Both these 1,000 years are symbolic amounts of time. The devil's happen FIRST and he gets out before the reign of Christ starts. We know Christ's 1,000 years are symbolic because the 2ⁿᵈ Resurrection happens just 6 verses down in 20:11-15.We also know it because the New Earth doesn't even come in until chapter 21, so Christ cannot be reigning on it. "A 1,000 years is with the Lord as a day & a day as 1,000 years".</u>

Verses 8-9 tell the same thing the devil did in chapter 16 as he goes to get others to help in the "Battle" *[war]. Gog & Ma-gog* **must be speaking of the devils 2 main human helpers, the 1ˢᵗ &**

2nd **Beasts. Verse 9 tells of their army surrounding the camp of the saints. Yes this is cloudy to me but we do see "saints" are still down here.** These are same saints of Daniel 7:25 & 12:17 [remnant] & "Vine of the Earth" 14:18. Where those Christians will be down here is not important to me. Most want to say they will be in Israel. That's ok with me because I don't plan to be here. Remember ALL even the blood Jews who did not accept Christ go to the Lake of Fire. Why God chooses this time to stop the devil is His business. It may be because Jesus said in **Rev. 2:23 "I will kill her children with death". So He is reserving that for Himself to do.**

Verses 10-15 show the devil being cast into the Lake of Fire; **"Where the beast & false prophet are". Showing the devil gets cast there shortly after the other 2.** We see the Great White Throne and the Father ready to judge. Verse 12 tells of a set of books being opened. Most say its books of each person's life on earth. It could be the Books of Law from the Bible because Christians were taken out from under the law. All fail when it comes to keeping the law, so all will go to the Lake of Fire. **But there's another book which is the book of life. If Jesus took His 7 verses earlier WHY open the book again?** Scholars say Gods just showing man He made no mistakes. **That's outrageous! God doesn't have to prove anything to us. There ARE names in that book of life. They are the names of the Saints CAST back who were found unworthy at the Judgment Seat of Christ.** They DID accept Christ while there was still time before the rapture. Now they will go to the New Earth, NOT heaven.

Verse 13 we see the **ALL COME OUT OF HELL. THAT'S SOMETHING NO ONE EVER HEARD BECAUSE THEY ALL JUST WENT ALONG WITH EVER THE PREACHERS TOLD US. "Death And HELL gave up the dead that were in them".** We see both death and hell being cast into the Lake of Fire. **And we see the other name for the Lake of Fire is; "THE SECOND DEATH".** Most will receive that 2nd death after they pay for all their sins in the lake. Some will be tormented longer, some shorter. The only ones humans who burn eternally with the devil & his angels are those who do the 3 things mentioned in Rev 14:9-11. We see the book of life mentioned again in verse 15 that it is checked for names. I truly believe that if Christians took the time to study carefully NOW these words they will understand it NOW. Stop letting someone else study for you. **Because there is one thing we must realize is that <u>NO EXCUSE WILL BE EXCEPTED AT THIS TIME.</u> No thinks their dumb and they aren't. But they will surly claim at this that they didn't know. What they really think is they will be able to con even GOD like they conned & lied their way through this world.**

"CHAPTER 21"

This chapter gives the details of the Holy City of Gold and WHO will dwell in it. It also tells of the New Earth and the Lake of Fire. We will see some verses are a repeat from earlier in Rev. Verses 1-3 shows a **"New Heaven & New Earth"**. So if the New Earth is just now coming in how can leaders say there is a 1,000 year reign on it? Both new places will be occupied by different sets of people. Remember the 7 plagues were poured on the old earth & all died. So God would not let us live down <u>there for 1,000 years. He doesn't make a new earth until now. John sees a **"Holy City" coming DOWN</u> from God OUT of Heaven"** [to the new earth]. **Verse 3 says; "The tabernacle of God is with men",** Meaning the humans on the New Earth. [They cannot go IN it]. **"God will dwell with them".** These are the same people from Rev. 7 that great number no man could count. Notice the wording that God will be WITH them [In Spirit]. This will be made clearer as go farther in this chapter.

Verse 4 really is a shocker; **"God shall wipe away all tears from their eyes".** We know that SAME verse from **7:17 & it is that same great number who went through Great Tribulation.** Who are these people crying their eyes out? Jesus said who would cry like that, those; **"Cast into outer darkness where will be weeping and gnashing of teeth ".** It is a good and happy event to go to heaven so we know God is not wiping tears from them. It's those who were cast back & went through literal hell. <u>**This chapter will switch from the earth bound**</u>

<u>people to those who will be In the Holy City & you must know who is who.</u> If any of you think for God to have a special set of people for Himself is wrong consider this. Jesus had 12 & 3 of them were closer than the others. In the Old Testament Numbers 18:20-21 & Deut.10:8-9 both say how God set apart the Levites & they had "No part nor inheritance with their brothers, but would only do service In the tabernacle". They did not get ANY of the land nor did any other work. <u>That is why they got a tithe from the other 12 tribes. They would never get rich or be well off. Compare that to these Pastors today.</u>

Verses 7-8 tell us of **"They that overcome shall inherit all things".** We know that from the 7 Churches & Jesus said this about those keeping HIS works. [I told you 2 sets of people would be switched back & forth & you must know who is who]. Verse 8 shows **those who went [already] to the lake of fire. No one comes out the Lake of Fire like they do hell. Notice who is the first mentioned before any of the 10 commandment sinner violators. "The fearful"; Why mention them first?** Christians CAN be lost for being scared. "God has not given us the spirit of fear". "Perfect love casts out fear". "In all these things we are MORE than conquerors". The devil will do his best to scare people & most all will fall for it. If we "Put on the whole armor of God" we won't have to worry about it. Then the verse goes on to mention the 10 commandment sins. Notice it says **"whoremongers"** instead of whores this time. The men who deal with whores are going to the same hell & it's about time they quit putting it on the woman. **The Lake of Fire is called the "SECOND DEATH" again!! Why people want to say this just means separation from God I don't know. God calls it death & it means death. They say separation because they saw it as people burning forever & ever and couldn't make this verse fit.**

Verses 9-21 we start to see the details of the **Holy City.** It is also called **the bride** because we are it, and we are married to Christ. **Rev**

3:12 **"I will make him a pillar in it".** We see again the city sits on a great & high mountain **ON the New Earth. Then it will go on to describe the absolute beauty of it.** It tells of the precious stones of all kinds. The 12 gates are **each 1 giant Pearl; angels are at each gate, and the names of the 12 tribes of Israel written at each gate. The City has 12 foundations & the names of the 12 Apostles are written on each of them. The City measured [in man's measurements] 1,500 miles square. Can you imagine the sight & brightness of it for all on the earth to see? We know they wished they had done different to be IN it. The City is pure gold like transparent glass. It is set with ALL manner of precious stones. [Why would any human not do all for this prize? They do all to win a lottery of millions in earthly money that will have NO value very soon].**

Verses 22-27 we get to some more shocking things that they Preach. Verse 22; **"I saw NO Temple therein". So when we saw in Rev 7:15 the great number no man could count wearing white robes also & it says; "They worship Him day and night IN His Temple" we know they are NOT IN this Holy City. This City is Heaven but sits on the Earth. They can <u>never come in it!!</u>** Verses 23-26 tell of those who are IN the City. It describes them as nations of them **saved. We must realize as of now we are ALL saved. But at the Judgment Seat of Christ we will see who DID hear Christ voice & did what He said. If they followed false preaching they will be cast back & not considered saved because truly saved means we are "saved from the wrath to come" Ro. 5:9 & 1 Thess. 1:10.** _If God had not put in place a chance for those who DID at least accept His Son but got fooled & tricked, there would be only those few millions saved, out of the billions that lived on this earth since the beginning._ We serve a great and merciful God who understands how lazy and hard headed we are. He gave us every tool to make it to Heaven and we can NOT blame Him.

Verse 27 tells us **"Nothing that defiles shall enter it".** We will cover just that right now. Remember In Rev 3:4 where Jesus is speaking to His Church. And even of them He says; "**Thou hast a FEW names…. Who have not defiled their garments**"? So how can people say they will be excused for getting it wrong? This verse tells us if we were defiled [like even those saved in 3:4 we will NOT get IN that City! Look who will get in; "Those whose names are written in the LAMBS BOOK OF LIFE" [and were not blotted out like the ones in 3:5]. Not the ones in the book of life in 20:12 & 15 either. The Lambs book is mentioned in 13:8 of those who did not fall for even the first beast or strike, like it says the whole world will do. Every year those on the New Earth MUST come up there to worship OUTSIDE that City. They cannot go in. Read of this in Is. 2:2-4 & Zach 14:16-19. Can you imagine those on earth coming up to that City & seeing its beauty all the time & knowing they could have been IN it? But they picked the wrong Pastor and Church to follow. They were too lazy to check for themselves.

I truly hope now you can see there are "2" books of life. One is the Lambs book". The Father will get the rest after Christ gets His; the best. Remember Jesus came to get a people for Himself & get a Kingdom for Himself. Jesus only Preached Heaven because we can all make Heaven.

I hope you see everything comes in 2's in Rev. 2 Tribulations; 2 Women; 2 Beast's; 2 notice the New Earth. And there is a difference these 2 eternal lives.

"CHAPTER 22"

This chapter is the conclusion of the whole Bible. It says no more about those on the New Earth, only what is happening in Heaven. It also gives us another insight into who the 2 Witnesses are. So let's start with verses 1-5. It speaks of a **"River coming from the Throne of God" right down the golden street. On each side of the river are 2 Trees of Life [no palm trees at all].** The water from this river flows by a mystery under a door in the temple that is **on the New Earth Ezekiel 47:1-4. Just like we have a Jerusalem as Heaven, those on earth will have an earthly Jerusalem. Ezekiel 40-48 tells of this earthly one.** Read about what the river does when gets to earth and the life it brings to all it touches. Our 2 trees in Heaven bear **12 different fruits every month. Notice the Father and the Son have a Throne in the City [where we are], and we serve him in it. Not like the ones in 7:15** who also "serve Him day & night in His Temple", because that is the earthly Temple. **And "We shall see His face". Remember Moses could not even see Gods face. God said; "No man can see his face and live". This proves we are no longer flesh but Spirit Beings like the angels.** People speak a lot on the 1,000 year reign, but our reign is really forever with Christ as He said in **2:26-27.**

Putting verse 6 with verse 16 we get a insight into the 2 Witnesses. "The Lord God of the Holy Prophets has sent His angel". 16 says; "I Jesus have sent Mine angel to testify THESE things In the Churches". *We know the God of the prophets means*

*Old Testament Prophets, meaning the Father. Then we see Jesus Himself sending someone also. The word angel here means "**messenger**".Look at the word Jesus uses; "testify". The only way you can testify is of things you saw and heard you SELF. Notice Jesus said "these" things. What things; the things written in Revelation of course. Who is the ONLY person who can testify to these? It is John only because he is the only one who SAW & HEARD them .It says again in verse 8 "I John saw & heard these things". All the way through this book John says; I saw & I heard. This also proves the point that in Rev. 10:10-11 when John is to eat the book & "He MUST prophesy AGAIN" that he is one of the 2 Witnesses. The other is Elijah from the Old Testament. Daniel gives us a mystery of these 2 in Dan. 12:5.it says; "I saw other 2; one on THIS side of the river & one on the OTHER side of the river". Let's figure this out this time without the scholars. Daniel 12 is speaking only on the last days. So these must be in our time. We must figure out what the "River" represents? When I pose this question I ask people; "what side of the river was Daniel on?"* They usually have trouble even with that. Daniel said "This side" meaning HIS SIDE. And the other one was on the OTHER SIDE. So Daniel is on the **Old Testament side & the other man is on the New Testament side. The river is symbolic for the division of the Testaments. It's like Jesus said; "If you can receive it". Doesn't that show perfect harmony of Old & New Testaments & the Father & the Son?**

Verses 8-15 John again is warned by the angel not to worship him. I said before in chapter 19 this happened & John was told this also. John as special as he is can BE LOST if he gets the big head of pride, as will we. **Proverbs 6:16-18 says "A proud look" is the number one thing God hates.** Verse 11 gives a finality to the whole thing by saying; **"Let them that are UNJUST or FILTHY or RIGHTEOUS or HOLY"; let him be that way STILL.** Meaning forever because it's too late now change anything. I love the way verse 12 reads; **"My reward is WITH Me".** You ever deal with someone who promised you or owed you and when you see them they say; "I got it, but it's at home; or in the bank etc.". Jesus said **"IT'S WITH ME". Verse 16 says; "Blessed are they that DO His commandments". Too many people talk a good game but won't DO anything. "This people draw near to Me with their mouth, and honor with lips, but their heart is far from Me".**

Verses 17-21 give us Gods Very last words of invitation to Salvation. Verse 17 uses the word "Come" 3 times". Everything is FREE, just COME. Then we get another warning about tampering with this book of Revelation. People have to tamper with it because they can't make it work with other last day scriptures. It will never fit with the rest of scripture on the last days their way. They have ALL the major events of this book wrong as 3 left shoes. I keep wondering what book they are reading. Are they changing it to keep their flock happy? Are they just guessing because they feel left out when they hear others guessing about Rev? Whatever it is it is YOUR life that's on the line also. Forget their reason. Now you have something to choose from. I showed you everything the educated master degree people say. I have no degrees.

"*HELL* FOLLOWED WITH *HIM*" REVELATION 6:8

This is one scripture has a point so great ALL should KNOW its meaning. Read the whole verse and pray about it. This is an event Jesus spoke of many times, yet NO one has made the connection. Now just from the title of this lesson we see that HELL is FOLLOWING the rider of the horse, and not alongside him. So the PALE rider gets there first. Then HELL comes shortly afterwards.

Where are they going?? It says plainly they are going to the EARTH!! Most people just assumed the hell was only for the DEAD. So why and how can hell be on earth with the living? Jesus said in MARK 9:43-48 "……THEIR worm dies NOT and the FIRE is NOT quenched". So these people are not dead physically yet. When Jesus spoke of the Rich man being in hell He said he was dead. So there is a hell for the dead AND one coming to earth for the LIVING at a certain time. Jesus would not have us ignorant of this event at this time because this will affect us. It was not necessary for those of old to know this because it was not going to affect them.

What makes it HELL here for the living? The unsaved dead have nothing to look forward to but the LAKE of FIRE at the 2nd Resurrection. They can never be saved because they did not accept Christ while they were alive. And at this time on EARTH the

7th Trumpet has sounded and the 1st Res. & Rapture have taken all who ever accepted Christ out of this world. REV. 10:6-7 says; "….there shall be time no longer"; <u>for what?</u> No more time for ANY human to accept Christ and be saved. So they are just like the dead from that moment on. Just like the DEAD they have no hope at all but to look forward to the LAKE of FIRE at the 2nd RES.!!!

Who is giving them this POWER?? Only GOD can grant such a thing, and HES giving it to the devil who is the rider of the horse. His name here is called DEATH, or the destroyer. Remember he "comes but to steal KILL and destroy".

Why is GOD doing this?? Before God raises all the dead of all the ages He is going to pour out His 7 vials of WRATH on this earth and every one left down here will, will, will die! If they escape the devils death, Gods plagues will kill them. And if the plagues don't kill them when Jesus comes back with those Saints who made the first RES. & the armies of Heaven for the War of Armageddon He will kill ALL left. Rev. 19:21.

What does the "4th part of the earth mean"?? Look at Daniel 2:40-43 and see he tells of a 4th Kingdom on the earth. Then look at verse 44; immediately after this kingdom come's Christ's Kingdom comes & will stand forever. Then look at Daniel 7:7, 19 & 23; it tells of a 4th Beast on the earth. Then in verse 29 it says also that Christ's Kingdom comes in forever. So we see now that the 4th part means the 4th or LAST time of the earth being run by SIN!!

Where does Jesus speak of these things and this TIME?? Every time He said "CAST them"; or GO YE" or "DEPART FROM ME", it is HIM Judging. Romans 14:10& 2 Corin. 5:10-11 both say Christians MUST ALL go to the Judgment Seat of Christ; if they did good or BAD…". This is where He will cast back ALL phony and mislead Christians to die with the Unsaved. But the best example of this time is "the Sheep and the Goats" in

Matt. 25:41 where He tells the Goats "Go ye into everlasting fire prepared for the devil and his angels". It is not the time for the devil to be punished yet but his last and short time for him to rule on earth before he is cast into the LAKE OF Fire forever. And at the 2nd Res, only those bad Christians cast back have a chance to get eternal life on the New Earth. Not Heaven. Because they did accept Christ in faith before the 7th trumpet sounded.

Other names for this time is ; OUTERDARKNESS; GREAT TRIBULATION; THE INDIGNATION; EVERLASTING FIRE; FURNACE OF FIRE; HOUR OF TEMPTATION; AND HELL for the LIVING!!! At this time the door to heaven will be shut so no prayers will get through.

ISN'T THIS A GOOD REASON To DOUBLE CHECK YOUR FAITH AND CHURCH? JESUS SAID; "MANY FALSE PROPHETS SHALL COME AND DECEIVE MANY". MANY MEANS "MOST". IF YOU ARE DOING WHAT THE MAJORITY OF SO CALLED CHRISTIANS ARE DOING YOU ARE MOST LIKELY IN THE WRONG!!!!!!!!

"JUDGE AND AVENGE OUR BLOOD" REV. 6:10

We can tell by the title that someone is in BIG trouble when the vengeance starts. We want to study this from verse 9-11. But first we will deal with just this. It is the saints who are asking GOD Himself to avenge their deaths. Because GOD said many times "...vengeance is mine said the Lord; I WILL repay". That means absolute and definite. If we believe in the rest of the Bible we should believe it when he says this. This is why Jesus said; "....if thy enemy hunger, feed him; if he thirst, give him to drink". Look at all the children of God who have died all the way from ABEL as Jesus put it, even to Stephen being stoned to death in Acts. And all the Apostles were killed except St. John.

Now let's start at verse 9. "I saw the souls of them under the altar who were slain for the Word of God and the testimony which they held" [on to]. These saints have not yet been resurrected at this time. It is as God said about ABEL's blood crying out to him from the earth after he was killed by his brother CAIN. And if can understand it; the ALTAR represents the earth.

Now we go to verse 10 and they say; "how long oh LORD Holy and True [to HIS WORD] does thou not judge and avenge our blood......" When God makes a promise He is faithful to keep it. "Heaven and earth shall pass away, but MY words shall not pass away". All over the Old Testament God tells of "IN THAT DAY". Yes he has chosen a day to lay the sin of all sinners back on their own heads. Now it says; "...ON THEM THAT DWELL ON THE EARTH". We see life is still going on, on the earth. And for some dumb reason no one knows that God is going to punish the sinners and the disobedient Christians together on the first earth. That's in Hebrews 10:26-30. Most don't even know when Christians go up in the Rapture they are going to be JUDGED to see if they are WORTHY to be ACCEPTED in that first resurrection. 2 Thess. 1:5 &11/ & Romans 14:19/ & 2 Corin. 5:10-11.

Now in verse 11 we see "white robes were given to them every one of them..." So with these white robes they are No longer in the graves, or no longer UNDER the ALTAR". Now they are told to; "...WAIT yet a LITTLE SEASON....." First let find what this LITTLE SEASON is?? The same word is in REV. 20:3. This same LITTLE SEASON is called a "SHORT TIME" in REV. 12:12, and a "...SHORT SPACE" in REV. 17:10. It is the SAME in all 4 places speaking of SAME time JUST BEFORE the RAPTURE!! All points to one MAJOR event which is when the devil is CAST down from Heaven AND he is OUT of the BOTTOMLESS PIT because his time there is finished. CAN WE NOW SEE HOW WRONG the scholars are when they say the devils 1,000 years bound are a future event!!

So they have their white robes, out of the graves and told to WAIT for WHAT???? "Till their fellow brothers and servants are KILLED _AS_ they were is fulfilled". Now remember in 1 Thess. 4 where it says; "...the dead in Christ SHALL rise FIRST, then we which are alive and remain shall be caught up with them...." Most can't see the word FIRST means a while before WE are going up, BUT NOT LONG AFTER!! Then the part about "...being killed AS they were....." Most of these were killed in the ROMAN PERSECUTION when the Apostles were killed. They will be watching us and praying for US to endure AS THEY DID!! This is where the Great falling away of 2 THESS. 2:3 will happen.

IT WILL BE A SAD, SAD DAY BECAUSE WE HAVE BEEN BOMBARDED WITH PREACHING THAT "WE" WILL NOT BE HERE WHEN THINGS GET BAD. THIS IS THE "MOST" HURTFUL TEACHING TO CHRISTIANS TODAY. IF GOD DID NOT SPARE THEM, WHY WILL HE SPARE US THIS TEST? CHRISTIANS TODAY ARE SOFT, AND WIMPS, AND DON'T WANT TO GO THROUGH ANYTHING. THEY THINK THEY WILL GO FROM LUXURY DOWN HERE TO LUXURY UP THERE. SO READ THESE SCRITURES BEFORE THE FIRST TRIB COMES ON US AND YOU ARE NOT ABLE TO HANDLE IT. IF YOU DON'T EXPECT IT, YOU WON'T BE ABLE TO ENDURE IT!!!

1. 1 CORIN. 3:13 "....THE FIRE SHALL TRY EVERY MANS WORK...."
2. REV. 2:10 "...YE SHALL HAVE TRIB. 10 DAYS...."
3. MATT. 24:29-31 & MARK 13:24-27"...IMMEDIATELY AFTER THE TRIB. OF THOSE DAYS....THEN SHALL YE SEE THE SIGN OF THE SON OF MAN COMING IN THE CLOUDS....AND GATHER HIS ELECT......."!!!!!!
4. REV.15:2 ON THE SEA OF GLASS WITH HARPS WERE THOSE WHO HAD; "...GOTTEN THE VICTORY OVER BEAST & HIS IMAGE..." ETC. MEANING THEY "WERE" DOWN HERE WHEN THEY WERE HERE!!!!

THE LAST THING IS THE SCRIPTURE THAT HAS FOOLED EVEN THE SCHOLARS. It is 1 THESS. 5:9 WHERE IT SAYS; ..."WE ARE NOT APPOINTED UNTO WRATH..." THIS IS THE WRATH OF GOD, NOT THE

FIRST TRIBULATION. THERE ARE 2 TRIBULATIONS. THE FIRST IS A TEST FOR ALL CHRISTIANS. THE SECOND IS CALLED THE "GREAT TRIB; WRATH OF GOD, OUTERDARKNESS, FURNACE OF FIRE; HELL; & THE INDIGNATION AND OTHER NAMES.

I TRULY PRAY CHRISTIANS WILL UNDERSTAND THIS BEFORE IT GETS HERE. MOST PASTORS OF TODAYS ARE "BLIND LEADING THE BLIND". DANIEL 11:33, 35 BOTH SAY "ONLY A FEW" WILL UNDERSTAND WHATS HAPPENING IN THESE LAST DAYS. NOT THE 200,000 PLUS SCHOLARS WHO WENT TO MANS SCHOOLS INSTEAD OF RELYING ON THE HOLY SPIRIT FOR THEIR INFORMATION.

"ABSOLUTELY"

What Happens At The Death Of Christian Backsliders!

THE BIBLE IS NO GUESING GAME AS TO WHAT HAPPENS TO ALL HUMANS AT DEATH. EVEN MOST PREACHERS DON'T UNDERSTAND THE SCRIPTURES ON THIS MATTER, OR JUST WANT TO KEEP THEIR FLOCK HAPPY REGARDLESS OF WHAT THE BIBLE SAYS. HERE ARE DIRECT SCRIPTURES ON THE SUBJECT AND YOU CAN CALL ME FOR MORE [323-587-7608]. *WE ALL KNOW MANY WHO WERE TRULY SAVED THEN FELL AWAY INTO SIN AGAIN BEFORE THEY DIED. SO HERE'S WHAT HAPPENS:*

ROMANS 14:10 & 2 CORIN. 5:10-11 BOTH SAY; "WE MUST ALL STAND BEFORE THE JUDGMENT SEAT OF CHRIST.." ONLY THOSE WHO EVER ACCEPTED CHRIST WILL BE HERE. IT ALSO SAYS: "WHETHER WE DID GOOD OR BAD"..IT ALSO SAYS IN VERSE 11: "KNOWING THEREFORE THE TERROR OF THE LORD". THIS IS THE PART PREACHERS DON'T TELL YOU.

1 CORIN. *15:51-52 & 1* THESS. 4:13-14 BOTH SAY: CHRISTIANS "SLEEP" TILL THE 1ST RESURECTION AND JUDGMENT SEAT OF CHRIST. WE DO NOT GO STRAIGHT TO HEAVEN YET, WE WAIT TILL THE RES.. THERE ARE ONLY 24 SAINTS IN HEAVEN RIGHT NOW SAYS REVELATION 4:4 & 5:8.

HEBREWS 10:26-29: " IF WE SIN WILLFULLY AFTER WE HAVE RECEIVED THE KNOWLEDGE OF THE TRUTH THERE REMAINS NO MORE SACRIFICE FOR SINS......BUT CERTAIN FEARFUL LOOKING FOR OF JUDGMENT & FIERY INDIGNATION WHICH SHALL DEVOUR THE ADVERSARIES........VS. 29; "HOW MUCH WORSE PUNISHMENT IS WORTHY FOR THOSE WHO TRAMPLE UNDER FOOT JESUS & THE BLOOD WHICH SANTIFIED HIM & DONE BAD TO THE SPIRIT OF GRACE". EXPLAINED IT IS THIS [WE ARE SAVED FROM THE WRATH OF GOD TO COME. IF WE SIN AFTER SALVATION WILLFULLY [BECAUSE WE ALL SIN] CHRIST SCARIFICE WILL NOT BE APPLIED TO US. WE WILL ABSOLUTELY BE CAST TO WHERE THE WRATH IS POURED OUT ON THE EARTH AND DIE WITH THE SINNERS LEFT STILL ALIVE DOWN HERE. EVERY HUMAN LEFT ON EARTH WILL BE KILLED, THE 2ND RES. WILL HAPPEN.

HEBREWS 12:5-7 SAYS THE SAME AS WHAT HAPPEN TO THE CHURCH THAT WAS SPIT OUT BY JESUS IN REV. 3:16 &19. "WHOM I LOVE I REBUKE AND CHASTEN". "IF WE ENDURE CHASTENING HE DEALS WITH US AS SONS". SO WE SEE EVEN THOUGH THEY WERE SPIT OUT THEY STILL HAVE A CHANCE FOR ETERNAL LIFE, BUT NOT IN HEAVEN. THEY WILL NEVER GO TO HEAVEN. THEY WILL GET THE NEW EARTH AND NEW HUMAN BODIES. THEY WILL NEVER ENTER THAT CITY OF GOLD WHERE GOD AND JESUS THRONE IS [REV. 21:27] EVERYWHERE THE JESUS SPAEKS OF CASTING OUT ANYTHING HE'S SPEAKING OF HIS JUDGMENT. THE SHEEP &

GOATS; WHEAT & TARES; LAZY SERVANT: DANIEL 12:3; ETC.

NOT ONLY CHRISTIANS WHO SIN WILL BE CAST OUT, BUT THE ONES WHO DON'T WITNESS OR BEAR FRUIT [JOHN 15:2]. THOSE WHO UNKNOWNINGLY FOLLOW FALSE TEACHING & [MATT. 15:14] & "MANY FALSE PREACHERS SHALL COME AND DECEIVE MANY". THOSE WHO ARE SELFISH WITH TIME & POSSESIONS [MATT. 25:31-45], & THOSE WHO'S FAITH FAILS BECAUSE OF FEAR OF DEATH OR ANY OTHER REASON BECAUSE OF WHAT THE BEASTS AND DEVIL WILL DO IN THESE LAST DAYS. BECAUSE NO RAPTURE HAPPENS TILL AFTER WE SEE THEM. [2 THESS. 2:3].

"THERE ARE 3 FIRES; ALL DIFFERENT"

Christians and the unsaved just assume that any FIRE Jesus spoke of is HELL. They also assume the LAKE of FIRE is the same as HELL. They also assume once a person is sent to any of them there is NO coming out ever!! But 2 of these fires people can come out of. So ask yourself these questions about these Scriptures; the ones Jesus spit out of His mouth in REV. 3:15-19 went to a FIRE. Why did Jesus tell them to repent if they could never come OUT???

1. 1 Corin. 3:14-15 says ONE shall receive a reward; the other CAN BE saved still if he goes through another FIRE.
2. Notice in 3:13 they BOTH go into a FIRE at first. Then they are judged and only one gets a reward. The other has to go through yet another FIRE to be saved from the 3rd FIRE which is yet to come which is the LAKE of FIRE!!!!!
3. What is the difference between the 2 FIRES in 13 &15; & what are their names?
4. Jesus never ever spoke of the LAKE OF FIRE because those who are APPROVED at His Judgment Seat will NOT have to endure any of the other 2 FIRES.
5. We will see numerous scriptures on the first 2 FIRES and what order they come! 1st FIRE=[test & regular Trib.] Then ;

6. 1st Res. & Judgment [Seat of Christ] 1,000 yr. reign begins in Heaven!! Then:

7. 2nd FIRE is;[Wrath & Great Trib. & Everlasting Fire & Furnace of FIRE & Out-Darkness]

8. 2nd Res. & Judgment [Great white throne of FATHER] Some REJECTED Christians from the 1st Res. Make it and get the NEW EARTH; NOT HEAVEN!! Then;

9. LAKE of FIRE is finally open for business. All left go to LAKE with No escape!!

10. If you were truly interested you would have checked the Bible about these questions before NOW. If you thought there was no need to study this YOU MAY be one of the MANY Christians who will have to go through that 2nd FIRE and maybe the 3rd!!

THE 1ST FIRE; or REGULAR TRIB.; or TEST

1 Corin; 3:13; Rev. 2:10; Matt: 7:24-27; 13:6-21, 30; 10:39; 20;6-7; 22:8-10; 24:29-31, 40-41. MARK 13:24; LUKE 14:16-23; 17:33; 21:8-19 &25-26; DANIEL 2:40-43; 7:19-24; 8:9-25; 11:29-35; 12:1-5 1ST THESS. 5:3-5; 2 THESS. 2:3-12; 1 PETER 4:12-17; ISAIAH 2:9-21; THERE ARE EVEN MORE THAN THESE ON 1ST FIRE. *THEN THE* 1ST RESURECTION & JUDGMENT SEAT OF CHRIST

2 CORIN; 5:10; ROMANS 14:10; MATT. 7:22; 13:30, 41-43, 48-49; 18:32-33; 20:8-9; 21:40; 22:11-12, 30 * 25: 19-29, 31-40; MARK 13:26-27; LUKE 12:36-38, 46; 14:24, 35; 21:27-28; JOHN 5:25 * 15:2, 6; 1 THESS. : 15-16; 2 THESS. 1:5, 11

HEBWS. 10:26-29; 1 PETER 4:18; 2 PETER 3:8; ISAIAH 26;19-20; 65:13-14; EZK.9:4; DANIEL 7:25; 12:2-3.

THEN WE HAVE THE 2ND FIRE; or WRATH of GOD; or GREAT TRIB; or HELL; or OUTERDARKNESS or EVERLASTNIG FIRE or FURNACE of FIRE. 1 CORIN. 3:15: 2ND CORIN 5:11; MATT. 7:23; 13:30, 42-43, 50 * 18:43; 20:10-16; 21:41; 22:12-13; 24: 50-51; 25:11-12, 30, 41-46; LUKE 12:47-48; 14:24; ISAIAH 61:6 62:2-3, 10; 65:9; DAN. 7:25; 11:36 & HEBWS. 10:27-31.

THERE ARE 2 OF THE 3 FIRES. THE "LAKE OF FIRE" IS THE LAST & NO ONE COMES OUT OF IT!

"OUTER DARKNESS; WEEPING AND NASHING OF TEETH"

Matthew 22:13

There are 5 places in Matthew alone. In each people are being CAST from one place to another. Our question is WHERE are they being cast FROM & where being cast TO? We know its HELL their being cast to. So we need to know WHY & who these people are. LET'S START WITH THE 5 SCRIPTURES.

1. Matt. 13: 42 "Wheat & Tares"; we see <u>good</u> and <u>bad in the same place &</u> being Judged [separated at same time].
2. Matt. 13: 47-51 "Net in Sea"; we see also <u>good & bad Judged [separated] at same time & place.</u>
3. Matt. 8:12 Just speaks of the Outer Darkness again.
4. Matt. 22:13 "Man with no Wedding Garment" also CAST BACK; [back because he somehow got all the way to where the wedding was to take place; then cast out BEFORE the wedding] . Notice also verse 10 good & bad there also.
5. Matt. 25:30 "Lazy Servant"; is cast to Outer Darkness. He was there with the Good Servants when judged UN worthy. NOW we see it is Very important to find out the WHO. WHERE & WHY about these 5 Scriptures so we won't be one of these Cast Out & Back!! Why don't Churches EVER Praech the "JUDGEMENT SEAT OF CHRIST"? They

think we Christians will just be raptured & go straight into Heaven. They may not see there is a STOP to make in the clouds where we will ALL be checked to see if we did what Christ Commanded Christians to do. So let me prove that these are Christian Believers who are being cast out [back] by more Scriptures.

1. Rev. 3:15-19; "Church of Laodicea" is SPIT OUT because they are LUKEWARM. Jesus does not sat they are not saved just they are casual, average, mediocre, & ordinary. If you are like other Christians you're LUKEWARM!!

2. Matt. 25:31-46; " Sheep & Goats"; Notice they are both together when they are separated cause they are Christians. Notice the Goats are sent to HELL yet none were said to violated a 10 Commandment like; lying, stealing, murder, fornication & adultery etc. Romans 6 tells us we are "Not under the Law" no Christian is. We are now under Christ's commands to do what He says. We will be judged by if we did what He said like these in these Scriptures we are Studying.

3. Ro. 14:10 & 2 CORIN. 5:10-11 Both say "we [Christians] must ALL stand before the judgment seat of Christ, if we did good or bad..". This is important because 3 of our Scriptures say "good & bad were together" when separated {judged]. We know there 2 Judgments & 2 Resurrections. No sinner goes to Christ's Judgment Seat; they go to the Great White Throne one in Rev. 20:11 at the 2nd Res.

"WHERE CAST FROM & WHERE TO"?

1. We see in 3 of our place's: Net in Sea--Wheat & Tares--Man No Wed Garment; they are TAKEN from the Earth [in the rapture] to somewhere in the air; clouds [1 Thess. 4:17] . Paul says "..so shall WE ever be with Lord'. Paul KNOWS who the WE are & it's not all. proof is;

2. 1 Corin. 3:14-15 Paul says; "he whose work abides [approved] shall receive a REWARD...he whose work is burned up [not approved] is saved but receives NO reward.

3. 2 Thess. 1:5 & 11 this same Paul says; "Pray ye be a*ccounted WORTHY of this calling".* Yes Paul knew & so do we need to know.

"WHY CAST OUT & BACK"?

We all know Christians who do not act anything like they should. They paly Christ for an all-day Sucker & think they will still get into Heaven. And the Pastors do not tell them different either to keep the offering big or the attendance big. Jesus told us exactly who He will cast out.

1. JOHN 15:2 "BARE NO FRUIT"; HEBS. 10:26-29 "SIN WILLFULLY"; REV. 3:16 LUKEWARM [AVERAGE]; MATT. 25:29-30 LAZY; & THEY WHO DO NOT ENDURE TO END [LOSE THEIR FAITH]

Let us always remember there will be NEW HEAVEN & NEW EARTH. WHO GOES WHERE IS UP TO US. We all know it's HELL they are being cast TO, at the 2nd. Res. REV.20:13 we see ALL came OUT of HELL, and the Book of life is open AGAIN. It is here those cast back go to the New Earth, and it is so many you can't even count them all. That's how many will get it wrong. Proof is;

<u>REV:7:9 & 14 & 17;</u> We see they went into Great Trib. which no obeying Christian will. This is their whipping & punishment NOT their final end. *VERSE 17 SAYS "GOD WILL WIPE THEIR TEARS [because they went to place Jesus said "weeping & gnashing of teeth].*

REV. 21:4; we see when the New Earth comes in God will "wipe away their tears" as 7:17.

REV. 3:19 JESUS says <u>*"who I love I rebuke & chasten"; ...REPENT.."*.</u> *He says repent because they still have a chance for eternal life on the New Earth Not Heaven if they get it wrong by False Preachers or whatever.*

REV: 14:16-19 TELLS THIS IN A SYMBOLIC WAY. READ IT WITH THIS INSIGHT & UNDERSTAND.

"STRIKE ONE; YOU'RE OUT" REVELATION 15:2 & 20:4

We know in baseball 3 strikes you're out. So what is this one strike here I am saying is Biblical? God said; "My thoughts are not yours & your ways not mine". Let's look first at these 2 scriptures. REV. 15:2; "Standing on the sea of glass them that got the victory over the beast & image & mark, and number of his name…having the harps of God". Notice the 3 things they overcame. REV. 20:4 "……..did not worship the beast or image or receive his mark…..and THEY lived & reigned with Christ 1,000 years". We see again the 3 things they overcame OR did not fall for.

So if they had fallen for even ONE of the 3 they would not be Reigning with Christ at the 1st Resurrection. Meaning they will not be going to Heaven. Notice also in Rev. 15:2 they have HARPS. It's important if you look at what the ones in Rev. 7:9 with white robes had in their hands; PALMS not HARPS. Palms shows they are getting the New Earth not Heaven cause there are NO Palm Trees in the Holy City only 2 Trees of Life on each side of the River of Life. Also notice Rev. 7:9 says in verse 7:14 what they had to go through before they got there. 14; " …came out of Great trib. & washed their robes…". We see in Rev. 2:20-23 that the Great Trib. Is a <u>PUNISHMENT</u> for Christians who fall for false teaching?

There is a trap here that will fool Christians before they come to the last 2 strikes [mistakes]. It's the 1st strike, and it comes years before the other 2. Rev. 13:8 "….and ALL that dwell upon the earth shall worship the beast whose names are not written in the LAMBS Book of Life…". [Rev. 21:27 speaking of those who are IN the Holy City it says names are written in the "LAMBS BOOK OF LIFE.."] At this time only the 1st beast is here the 666 guy and he brings peace & prosperity to the earth which will cause even mislead Christians to think he is someone special. Worship does not mean bowing down only thinking in their heart he is some good & great person. In reality he is the devils front man. 13:7 says; "…he makes war with the Saints…". It is only the SMALL Group of Real Christians he is making war with. The majority following false teachings and are not bothered by him. This will give the majority a sense of being in the right with Christ. It will not be till the 2nd beast comes in, in 13:11 and makes the Image & makes it talk & makes a law to worship it or die that they will see they were worshiping the wrong person!!! BUT NOW THEY HAVE THAT FIRST & ONE STRIKE WHICH MAKES THEM "NOT" ELIGIBLE FOR HEAVEN PERIOD. As I said before this first mistake comes 1-2 years before the 2nd 2 strikes. Oh how foolish & bad they will feel that they can no longer get Heaven. But they do have a chance at the New Earth & are that Great multitude in Rev. 7:9 & 14.

They were warned and should have known better because Rev 11:3-7 & 14:1-5; the 2 Witnesses & 144,000 told them before this came. But they decided to stay with their particular Denominational Teachings. They followed the "Tradition of the Elders" & are the "Vine of the Earth" Rev.14:18. They were NOT lead by Christ's Holy Spirit. John 10:5 & 27 "..strangers they will NOT follow & MY sheep hear MY voice". Matt. 24:24; : "….false prophets arise & do great signs & wonders that "IF" it were "POSSIBLE" would fool the very elect". So we see who can NOT be fooled is real Christians who conform to Jesus words regardless of what the Scholars & Majority of Churches teach. We don't mind being "FEW" in number. Rev. 3:4 "…thou has a FEW names even in Sardis who have not defiled their garments".

Matt. 7:14 "...narrow is way to life & FEW find it". Yes that great number with white robes in Rev. 7:9 & 14 are NOT the ones who got it right but got it WRONG!!! No Jesus will not forgive false teachers OR those who believe them. Matt. 15:14 "..if the blind lead the blind BOTH fall....". Why is that number so big that "..NO MAN COULD COUNT THEM..."? Of the 2 Billion professed Christians living today [IF you count the Catholic's] only 10% will believe the 2 Witnesses God & Jesus are sending [Rev. 22:6 &16] to help us correct the numerous False Doctrines we have today.

Let's sum this up with the difference between these 2 groups of Christians, because Yes they are saved. Rev. 3:4 "...I will not BLOT out his name from the book of life..". No one Church ever taught your name can come OUT the book just like it went IN. Isaiah 60:14 & 66:14 "...all they that despised thee shall come BENDING down unto thee..". "...your brethren that HATED you....He shall appear to your Joy but they shall be ashamed". Rev. 3:9 "...I shall make them of the Synagogue [church] of satan who say they are Jews [Christians] to come & worship at thy FEET & know I loved THEE [not them]." Daniel 12:2 "... some to everlasting life, some to SHAME & everlasting contempt".

It was the Religious Leaders through history who gave Gods people the most trouble & even killed Jesus & the Prophets. The same will happen in these last days. The False Prophet & mislead Christians will HATE & do all manner of evil against the FEW true Christians. The Leaders will not change & admit they Preached wrong. They will take their whole Church to hell with them rather than admit it. It's up to YOU to stand with Christ or the majority. Yes they will stop following the False ones but only when the 2nd & 3rd strikes come in and it's too late to make Heaven!!! Remember ALL Christians names are in Jesus book NOW, but at His Judgment Seat [Ro. 14:10 & 2 Corin. 5:10-11] all who got it wrong, names will be blotted out. Bro. Fred Smith

"THE 2 HELLS"

JESUS SPOKE OF 2 HELLS, ONE FOR THE THOSE WHO DIE, AND THE OTHER FOR THE LIVING, WHERE THEIR WHOLE BODY IS CAST THERE AND "THEIR WORM DIETH NOT". THE FIRST HELL IS WELL KNOWN IN THE PARABLE OF THE "RICH MAN AND LAZARRUS" IN LUKE 16:19-31. IN IT JESUS WANTS US TO SHOW US HE WAS "DEAD AND BURIED". IN THE GRAVE THE BODY DECAYS AND THE WORMS EAT ALL THE FLESH, LEAVING ONLY THE BONES AND TEETH. VERSE 23 SAYS; "IN HELL HE LIFTED UP HIS EYES BEING IN TORMENTS". NOTICE IT SAYS TORMENTS BEFORE IT SAYS "FLAME" IN VERSE 24.

WE HAVE BEEN TAUGHT FOR CENTURIES THAT HELL IS FOREVER, AND IN A REAL FIRE. WE KNOW FIRE HURTS FLESH, BUT DOES IT HURT A SPIRIT ALSO? SO WHAT IS THIS TORMENT AND FLAME? THE J. H. WITNESS TEACHES THERE IS NO MEMORY OR HURT AFTER OUR DEATH. BUT IN GENESIS 4:10 GOD SAYS TO CAIN AFTER HE KILLED HIS BROTHER ABLE; "THY BROTHERS BLOOD CRIES OUT TO ME FROM THE GROUND". THIS IS NOT A PARABLE. THERE IS A LIVING PART OF US AFTER THE BODY DIES. IT HAS A REFF. TO REV. 6:10 WHERE THE SAINTS SPEAK FROM THE GRAVE

SAYING; "HOW LONG WILL THOU NOT AVENGE OUR BLOOD ON THEM ON THE EARTH".

SALVATION IS FOR THE LIVING TO ACCEPT ONLY. THE DEAD HAVE NO CHANCE OR HOPE LEFT AT ALL PERIOD. AND THE LIVING SOUL OR SPIRIT LEFT OF THEM KNOWS THIS FACT. THE RICH MAN WANTED TO WARN HIS BROTHERS NOT TO COME THERE. THE ONLY WAY FOR THEM NOT TO GO THERE IS TO ACCEPT CHRIST WHILE "ALIVE"!!!

WE HAVE HEARD OF "BURNING" WITH LUST, LOVE, ANGER, HATE, AND GUILT ALSO BURNS IN US. THE RICH MAN WAS TORMENTED BY A BURNING GUILT AND REGRET OF BEING IN A HOPELESS, HELPLESS, UNCHANGING STATE OF THE JUDGMENT AND DOOM THAT HE KNOWS WILL SURELY COME. HE WILL FACE GOD THE FATHER AT THE SECOND RESURECTION, BECAUSE HE REJECTED CHRIST AND SALVATION. AND HE KNOWS HIS FATE IS THE "LAKE OF FIRE". THIS IS A TORMENT.

THE NEXT HELL JESUS SPOKE OF IS ONE WHERE THE WHOLE BODY IS CAST AND HE SAYS: "THEIR WORM DIETH NOT". WORMS EAT DEAD BODIES AND LEAVE BONES AND TEETH ONLY. IN MATT; 5:29-30 & MARK 9:43-48 JESUS TELLS OF THIS HELL. CUTTING OFF YOUR HANDS OR PLUCKING OUT YOUR EYES MEANS DON'T LET ANYONE OR THING GET YOU SENT THERE. NO RELATIVE, FRIEND, OR PREACHER. "CUT THEM OFF AND CAST THEM FROM YOU" HE SAYS. WHO DO YOU LOVE MORE????????

THIS HELL FOR THE LIVING HAS NOT COME YET. BUT IT TELLS OF THIS IN REV. 6:8. THIS RIDER IS THE DEVIL CALLED DEATH OR THE DESTROYER.

"AND HELL FOLLOWED WITH HIM", TO EARTH!! IT SAYS FOLLOW BECAUSE SHORTLY AFTER THE DEVIL ARRIVES THE 7TH TRUMPET BLOWS;WHEN PAUL SAYS CHRISTIANS WILL BE TAKEN OUT OF THIS WORLD [1 CORIN 15:51-52]. NOTICE REV 11:7 THE DEVIL KILLS THE 2 WITNESSES, AND THE 7TH TRUMPET BLOWS IN VERSE 15. THEN IN REV 10:6-7 IT SAYS "TIME SHALL BE NO MORE". MEANING NO ONE CAN BE SAVED AFTER THAT, BECAUSE WE ARE SAVED BY FAITH AND WHEN THEY SEE US GO THERE IS NO MORE FAITH INVOLVED. YET THE SINNERS ARE STILL ON EARTH WAITING FOR THE WRATH OF GODS 7 PLAGUES TO BE POURED OUT.

ANOTHER THING WE NEED TO KNOW IS ABOUT THE WORD "EVERLASTING". IT MEANS "AS LONG AS IT LASTS IN SOME PLACES. IN 2 PETER 2:4 AND JUDE 6 WE SEE ANGELS BOUND IN EVERLASTING CHAINS UNTO [UNTIL] THE JUDGMENT". SO THEY DON'T STAY THERE FOR EVER AND EVER BUT "UNTIL" THE GREAT WHITE THRONE JUDGMENT AT THE SECOND RESURECTION. SO WHEN JESUS MENTIONS "EVERLASTING FIRE HE'S SPEAKING OF THR FIRE OF THE GREAT TRIB. WHICH HAPPENS "BEFORE" THAT 2ND RES. JUDGMENT WHEN ALL THE REST GET UP AND GO TO THE LAKE OF FIRE. AND TO ADD ONE MORE THING; IN REV. 14:9-11 TELLS WHAT HUMANS "WILL" BURN FOREVER AND EVER IN THE LAKE OF FIRE. IT'S THE ONES WHO RECEIVE THE "MARK OF THE BEAST ONLY". THE REST WILL ONLY HAVE "THEIR PART THERE BEFORE THEY DIE THE SECOND DEATH ACCORDING TIO REV. 21:8.

THE BILLIONS LEFT HERE WILL BE JUST LIKE THE DEAD "NOW"; "NO MORE HOPE OR CHANCE" OF SALVATION. THEY HAVE A CERTAIN, SURE AND

UNCHANGEABLE FATE OF THE 2ND RESURECTION AND THE "LAKE OF FIRE". IMAGINE THE MENTAL TORMENT OF THAT SITUATION, PLUS THE WARTH OF GOD BEING PUORED OUT ON EARTH. IT'S HELL FOR THE LIVING. IN THE PARABLE OF THE VIRGINS IT SAYS; "THE DOOR TO HEAVEN WAS SHUT". NO MORE PRAYERS GETTING THROUGH AND DEVIL IS IN CHARGE. THIS IS THE SAME AS MATT. 25: 41; "PREPARED FOR THE DEVIL AND HIS ANGELS " [TO RULE DOWN HERE: NOT BE PUNISHED]. REV 12:12 TELLS OF THIS ALSO; "HE KNOWS HE HAS BUT A SHORT TIME". IN REV. 6:8 IT'S CALLED THE "4TH PART OF THE EARTH", MEANING THE LAST TIME OF THE EARTH. IN MARK 9 WHERE IT SAYS "THE FIRE SHALL NOT BE QUENCHED", MEANS SINCE THE DOOR TO HEAVEN IS SHUT SO NO HELP WILL COME AT ALL PERIOD.

THERE ARE OTHE NAMES FOR THIS TIME OS THE LIVING HELL. THEY ARE:

OUTER DARKNESS; MATT 22:13 & 25:30. EVERLASTING FIRE; & MATT 25:41. FURNACE OF FIRE; MATT 13:50 & HELL-MATT 5:29-30 & MARK 9:43-48 GREAT TRIB.-REV.2:22. INDIGNATION; ISAIAH 26:20 & HEBREWS 10:27; DANIEL 11:36 & HEBREWS 10:27.

CHRISTIANS JUDGED UNWORTHY AT THE JUDGMENT SAET OF CHRIST WILL BE CAST BACK HERE ALSO. DANIEL 7:25/ REV. 14:17-19/ MATT 25:41 & 1 CORIN. 3:15. THIS IS THE "SORER PUNISHMENT" SPOKEN OF IN HEBREWS 10:29. JUST AS GOD CAN CHANGE US IN MOMENT, HE CHANGE US BACK AND SEND US BACK IN MOMENT ALSO. PAUL SAYS IN 2 CORIN 5:10-11. 2 CORIN.

5:10-11 "KNOWING THEREFORE THE TERROR OF THE LORD….". VERSE 10 SAYS EVEN BAD CHRISTIANS WILL GO UP TO BE JUDGED. WHY CHURCHES TEACH THEY WILL ALL STAY UP IS BEYOND ME. WHEN JESUS SAID MANY TIMES "CAST THEM; CAST THEM"; WHERE DO THEY THINK THOSE PEOPLE WERE BEING CAST FROM?????

"SO WE BOILED MY SON, AND DID EAT HIM"

2 Kings 6:29

This is one of the harshest scriptures in the Bible. Yet someone must tell it. The story behind this verse starts at verse 24, so read it from there. It has a much broader meaning even for us today. This event is a SIEGE that happened in 893 BC., by the Syrian Army. It also happened in 588 BC by the Babylonians, and 70 AD by the Romans. Each of these God warned Israel to repent to avoid it. In the Roman siege of 70 AD Jesus warned while on the Cross; [Luke 23:28 "...weep not for Me, but weep for yourselves and your CHILDREN".

This Bible study has 2 major points that ALL should know and tell others with children. If they don't care enough about their own life they may care about their children more. Because there is another SIEGE coming up and it's called the GREAT TRIBULATION. A siege is to be locked in a place with NO means of anything coming in or going out. That means FOOD and WATER also. These Armies even built walls around the CITY to make sure no one could escape. They did not just attack and kill, they made them suffer first. So when the food ran out babies were first as very tempting food.

Ezekiel 14:13-18 God says when He sends destruction "though these 3 men were in it, Noah, Daniel & Job;. They shall deliver neither sons nor daughters, but they only shall be delivered THEMSELVES"

When the Rapture comes ONLY the CHILDREN of the SAVED will

leave this earth. Acts 16:31 "… thou shall be saved AND thy HOUSE". And that is only those too young to accept Christ for themselves. [Teenagers & up will be doomed unless they are saved for themselves]. The whole earth will be under GODS SIEGE after the Rapture. And he tells what He will do to ALL left down here in Revelation chapter 16. So let's look at the first 4 Plagues poured out on the earth. # 1 IS BODILY SICKNESS FOR THOSE WITH THE MARK OF THE BEAST. #2 IS EVERY LIVING THING DIES IN THE OCEANS. #3 IS ALL FRESH WATER IS TURNED TO BLOOD [MADE UNDRINKABLE]. # 4 IS THE SUN BURNS HUMANS WITH "GREAT" HEAT.

60% of the world's food comes from the sea. So with nothing to eat from the sea starvation is on the way fast. Then there will be no more fresh water to drink for humans or animals.

Then the SUN starts getting very, very hot every day. With animals dead all over the earth, and forests the smell of rotting flesh and fish will cause a horrible smell and odor all over the earth. That is the 7th Plague in 16:17. So how long do you think it will take for every human on earth to die? [About 6 months]. But Jesus will come back here to fight the WAR of ARMAGEDDON. At that time He will kill HIMSELF everyone [Rev. 19:11-14 &21] left alive. At the 2nd Resurrection in 20:11-15 we see only DEAD people are rising because no one is left alive by then.

When parents are saved their children are sanctified also because of the parent's salvation. But the unsaved parents' children are not. Children died in each of those SIEGES, and in the FLOOD of NOAH's day. Yes during the Great Trib. People will curse GOD because of their children's suffering and their own. They may gamble with their own salvation but not with their children's. Christians following False Doctrine and Pastors will double think it now or they will be cast back also.

So let the scary Pastors and Leaders only tell the NICE parts of GODS Word. God does have some down here who will tell it ALL. As Paul said in Acts 20:26 "…I am FREE from the blood of all men, for I have not shunned to declare unto you ALL the counsel of GOD"!!!!!!!!

DID JESUS TRY TO CHICKEN OUT????

If the leader of a gang tried to chicken out when things got rough for "him", why should he expect his followers to do any better? We look to our leaders for strength. If they fail to show it, where does that leave us? Everything Jesus told the 12 came absolutely true for 3 + years. The 12 were the ones being left in leadership & of saving the world. IT WAS JESUS WHO SAID;

"FEAR NOT THEM WHO KILL THE BODY". "HE THAT WILL SEEK TO SAVE HIS LIFE SHALL LOSE IT". "BE FAITHFUL UNTO DEATH, AND I WILL GIVE YOU A CROWN OF LIFE". REV. 12:13:11 "THEY LOVED NOT THEIR LIVES UNTO THE DEATH". THE LIST GOES ON AND ON!!!

SO WHY DO CHURCHES SAY JESUS WAS TRYING TO AVOID DEATH WHEN HE SAID: "FATHER IF IT BE POSSIBLE, REMOVE THIS CUP"???? LET'S CHECK THIS FURTHER.

We are much weaker than He was. He was full of the Holy Ghost. He knew He would go back to heaven to rule. So why didn't people look deeper into this issue? If He tried to chicken out, we don't have much chance at all. Most Churches and pastors don't realize this is what they are saying about Him. LET'S CONSIDER THIS AGAIN

1. *Everything Jesus told the 12 for 3 + years came absolutely true.*
2. *The 12 were the ones being left in leadership charge of saving the*

world. *Checking just BEFORE [then AFTER] this statement was made.*

3. *We look at the 3 Gospels first of this event in Matt. 26:31-42; Luke. 22:37-42; and Mark 14:27-36 with the key verse 33;*

4. *Jesus told them; "…they will smite the Shepard and the sheep will scatter".*

5. *They said; "No we won't". Or; Jesus you are wrong. Or; Jesus that not happen.*

6. *Now notice ALL these verses use the word "THIS CUP", not THE CUP.*

7. *Jesus is NOT saying "remove THE cup of death, but ONLY "THIS" one.*

8. *And ONLY remove it THIS TIME, NOT forever!!!! WHY? WHY? WHY?*

9. *Because He saw they still were not ready to take over yet. They still did not get it. If they had they would have accepted His saying of them scattering.*

10. *Now is there PROOF of this???*

11. *In Marks version of this in 14:33 "…He began to be SORE [hurt] and AMAZED [surprised & shocked] and very heavy".*

12. *The whole world depends much on these 12 and He is about to leave this earth. And they still question what He says.*

13. *So He was asking the Father for more time to teach "them". Not to spare his own life. {chicken out]*

14. *He came to this earth to die for us. He knew if He did not die no human would be saved at all ever. He wanted to do this because He loved US so much.*

15. *More proof is John's version of this event. Notice the scripture BEFORE is "they will smite the Shepard and the sheep will scatter". The event AFTER is JUDAS bringing in the multitude to take Jesus.*

16. ***John has BETWEEN verses John 16:32 and 18:1-3 a long PRAYER in Chapter 17.

17. It is a prayer for the 12 ONLY. NOT FOR HIS OWN LIFE!!!!

18. It is said they all feel asleep. But John must have woke up to have recorded this prayer BEFORE Judas brought the multitude.

19. God was saying "I'll take care of them but you [Jesus] come on home.

20. Jesus got no more time, nor will WE get more time. The end will be the END.

21. Let Pastors & Churches wrongly divide this and think Jesus was trying to chicken out. We NOW know the TRUTH!

"3 STRIKES YOU'RE OUT & IMAGE TO THE BEAST"

Revelation 13:15-16

IN REV. 13:15 IT SAYS THE IMAGE WILL <u>BOTH</u> SPEAK <u>AND.</u> SO WE SEE THE IMAGE WILL DO MORE THAN JUST SPEAK. SO WHAT ELSE IS IT DOING?? IT WILL; "CAUSE THAT AS MANY AS WOULD NOT WORSHIP THE IMAGE [ITSELF] SHOULD BE KILLED". AND THE NEXT VERSE SAYS THIS SAME IMAGE IS THE ONE WHO IS; "CAUSING ALL TO RECEIVE A MARK THAT NO ONE CAN BUY OR SELL WITHOUT THE MARK". SO WE ARE SEEING THAT ONCE THE IMAGE GETS LIFE FROM THE 2ND BEAST OF 13:11 IT IS THE IMAGE OR IDOL WHO IS CALLING THE SHOTS FROM THEN ON. NOT THE 1ST OR 2ND BEAST, BUT THE IDOL WHO WAS GIVEN LIFE. GOD SAID ALL THROUGH THE BIBLE THAT "NO IDOL COULD SEE, HEAR, WALK OR TALK". NOW IT LOOKS LIKE GOD IS A LIAR OR THIS IMAGE "IS" GOD. FOR THE IMAGE TO TALK IT MUST BE THINKING ALSO. IT HAS A LIFE OF ITS OWN. AT THIS TIME THE 2 WITNESSES ARE DEAD AND MOST OF THE WORLD DID NOT BELIEVE THEM OR THE 144,000'S PREACHING. SO 2 THESS 2:11-12 KICKS IN WHERE GOD SAYS; "FOR THIS CAUSE GOD WILL SEND THEM STRONG DELUSION THAT THEY SHOULD

BELIEVE A LIE, THAT THEY ALL MIGHT BE DAMNED".
REMEMBER THE BIBLE SAYS; "IT'S NOT GODS WILL
THAT ANY SHOULD PERISH". BUT AT THIS TIME GOD
IS SAYING FORGET IT, AND THEM ALL WHO HAVEN'T
BELIEVED BY THEN.

NOW THE 8TH KING
OF REV. 17:10-11

THE LAST 2 KINGS ON THE 7 HEADED BEASTS ARE THE 2 BEASTS OF REV. 13:1 & 11. THE BEAST ONLY HAS 7 HEADS. SO WHO IS THIS 8TH HEAD THAT IS RUNNING THINGS NOW? IT IS THE IMAGE. AND GUESS WHO IS IN THE IMAGE DOING THE SPEAKING??? IT IS SATAN HIMSELF. SATAN IS A SPIRIT AND HE HAS NO BODY. HE DOES INDWELL THE OTHER 2 BEASTS BUT NO ONE CAN DO HIS JOB BETTER THAN HE HIMSELF. JUST LIKE HE SPOKE THROUGH THE SNAKE TO EVE IN THE GARDEN OF EDEN, HE WILL BE SPEAKING THROUGH THIS HAND MADE IDOL. THIS IS WHY REV. 17:11 SAYS' HE IS OF THE 7" KINGS BECAUSE HE CONTROLED THEM ALL WHEN THEY WERE IN POWER THROUGHOUT HISTORY ANYWAY, ALL THE WAY BACK IN HISTORY. NOW TO UNDERSTAND WHAT THE "WAS AND IS NOT" MEANS IS THIS. REV. 17:8 SAYS IT LIKE THIS; "THE BEAST THAT WAS AND IS NOT, AND YET IS". _THE DEVIL WAS HERE ON EARTH MANY THOUSANDS OF YEARS. SOMEWHERE IN THE PAST SYMBOLIC 1,000 YEARS HE WAS BOUND IN THE BOTTOMLESS PIT [REV. 20:1-3]. [IS NOT HERE NOW] HE IS LET OUT AT THE 5TH TRUMPET IN REV. 9:1-2. AT THE TIME THE 2 WITNESSES AND 1ST BEAST ARE HERE_

IS DURING THE 6TH TRUMPET THAT STARTS IN REV. 9:13. BUT THE DEVIL ISN'T ALLOWED BACK DOWN HERE ON EARTH TILL REV. 12:9-13, ["YET IS" HERE AGAIN]. NOTICE HOW 13 SAY'S:" WHEN HE SAW HE WAS CAST INTO THE EARTH". EVEN HE IS SURPRISED HE IS BACK ON THE EARTH. AND IT SAYS "HE KNOWS HE HAS BUT A SHORT TIME". THE"ABOMMINATION THE MAKETH DESOLATE" IS WHEN THEY MAKE THE IMAGE SHORTLY AFTER HE GETS BACK & WAS SPOKEN OF IN DANIEL 12:11 & MAT 24:15.

"3 STRIKES YOU'RE OUT"

REV. 14:9-11 TELL US IF A PERSON DOES 3 SEPARATE THINGS THEY WILL BE "TORMENTED FOR EVER AND EVER, AND HAVE NO REST DAY AND NIGHT FOREVER". AND THIS IS IN THE LAKE OF FIRE NOT HELL!! SO THE OPPOSITE OF THIS IS THOSE WHO DON'T DO THESE 3 THINGS WILL NOT; I SAY NOT BE TORMENTED FOREVER IN THE LAKE OF FIRE. THEY WILL RECEIVE THE 2ND DEATH SPOKEN OF IN REV. 20:6 & 2:11 & 21: 8.THOSE WHO NEVER ACCETED JESUS WILL GO THERE TO BE PUNISHED FOR THEIR SINS ON THE EARTH. THOSE WHO DID MORE AND WORSE SINS WILL SUFFER LONGER. THOSE WHO DID LESS SINS WILL SUFFER LESS. "WHATSOEVER A MAN SOWETH THAT SHALL HE ALSO REAP". "SOME SHALL BE BEATEN WITH MANY STRIPES, SOME WITH FEW STRIPES". THIS IS WHAT REV. 21:8 MEANS WHEN IT SAYS, "SHAL HAVE "THEIR PART" IN THE LAKE OF FIRE". THE WORSHIP OF THE 1ST BEAST COMES WAY BEFORE THE IMAGE IS EVEN MADE. REV.13:8. ALL BUT THE REAL CHRISTIANS WILL WORSHIP HIM, BUT THAT ALONE IS JUST STRIKE ONE. THEN COMES WORSHIPPING THE IMAGE AND IF THEY DO THAT IT'S STRIKE TWO. NEXT IS THE "MARK" AND THAT IS STRIKE 3 THEY "WILL" BE TORMENTED FOR EVER & EVER WITH THE DEMONIC ANGELS.

THEY HAD THE PROHETS IN THE OLD TESTAMENT AND JESUS & THE APOSTLES IN THE NEW. THEY HAVE THE HOLY SPIRIT NOW. IF THEY DON'T BELIEVE THE 2 WITNESSES, AND THE 144,000 THAT ARE SOON TO COME; 2 THESS 2:11-12 WILL KICK IN. "GOD WILL SEND THEM STRONG DELUSION THAT THEY SHOULD BELIEVE A LIE THAT THEY ALL MAY BE DAMNED". IT'S BETTER TO DIE RIGHT NOW THAN BE HERE WHEN THE MARK LAW COMES AND YOU ARE TO FEARFUL TO RESIST IT. PEOPLE WANT TO LIVE, EVEN IF IT'S JUST FOR ANOTHER DAY OR MONTH. BUT JESUS SAID; "HE WHO WILL SEEK TO SAVE HIS LIFE SHALL LOSE IT".

"FINAL THOUGHTS"

Many times in this book I speak of double checking what we have been taught in whatever Denomination we were raised in. With so, so much at stake why not take that time? Anything passed from person to person can end up much different than what was first said. From Malachi to Matthew was 400 years of basic silence from God with no prophet being sent till John the Baptist & Jesus? Look how far off track the Religious leaders had taken Temple worship & added and subtracted laws calling them Gods Laws. Which side did Jesus take? Which side did Jesus say was right? NONE! It's been 2,000 years now since a Prophet was sent to earth. How far off track do you think the Church has gotten **today? Isaiah Chapter 5 gives a story about a "Vineyard". God said He watered it, & did everything else** for "HIS" vineyard, yet it produced "WILD [sour] GRAPES". He said He would; "Tear down that vineyard and start over". Do you see sour Christians today in great, great numbers? Do you watch the news? Which Church today would "you" say is right? Don't you believe God can start over today with True Preaching & save many from false doctrine so they can make Heaven & not just the New Earth? **EVERY BAPTIZED believer "IS" saved! All that needs to be done is bring them "OUT" of false doctrine!** We can go to ANY Church that is not too far off track. We will be judged by who our Faith is truly IN? If we "JOIN" a Denomination we are saying in effect "we believe that one IS the right one, and all others are not". <u>Go to anyone but claim only</u>

<u>**Christ & tell others this!**</u> You don't have to UN join, just **"in your heart UN join & tell others this"**.

How can we be a serious, productive witnesses for Christ to other world religions by telling them to re-check what they believed thousands of years, and we won't double check what we been in only a few generations? I cannot stress enough <u>**Ezekiel 9:4 "Set a mark on them that sigh and cry for the abominations being done", in the Temple [Churches} today.**</u> If you can't SEE it & think everything is pretty much OK your heart is **"far from Christ's"**. **He warned us over and over that "many false Leaders would come and deceive many"**. It's not just Revelation they have wrong. Did you know the majority of Jesus Parables have a last day Revelation message??? The "Sheep & Goats" are BOTH Christians yet one is cast out. When have you ever heard that? I should have done a book on the connection between the Parables & Revelation.

Before ANY of this can work for you, you MUST be keeping away from SIN. Not the ones man brought in but the big **"10"**. **I know "we" are not under the Law but we never violate the 10.** Study Romans 14 and see we do have a lot of freedom IN Christ. 14:14 says **some** things can be a SIN for one and NOT the other. Christ will take care of our other weaknesses of ill behavior. All he asks of is; **"Do some WORK to save as many as we can before the very soon coming END". We don't work to be saved we work BECAUSE WE ARE SAVED!!!!**

I will leave off here and just pray for all who read this book. I pray for all who are going to step out of the majority into the minority & be on that "narrow way that leads to life & [very] few find life". There are "2" tribulations & we "all" are going into the first one, so don't be caught unprepared or you will be one those Paul spoke of in 2 Thess. 2:3; "a falling away first". God did not let this slip up on you, your pastors tried to let it slip up you. LEARN HOW THE HOLY SPIRIT LEADS; HE STILL LEADS!!

eHH

Everyone who knows Bro. Fred is wondering how he gets these insights on the Last Days none of them even considered while reading the same scriptures. When he explains what's right there you can finally see the picture. He speaks in everyday language so the common person can understand it. The amazing thing is he has no Bible training & even less regular schooling. He takes & sends these to many Pastors & Scholars to check for errors if there be any. None have ever found a flaw they dared to challenge him on. He has asked them; "why do you Preach otherwise on Revelation"? Again they have no answer. Jesus said; "I will give you a mouth & wisdom they will not be able to gainsay nor resist". Paul said; "The Gospel he preached he neither received it from man nor was taught it, but by the Holy Spirit". Why do Christians today think we MUST go mans Bible Colleges to learn Gods Book? Jesus & His 12 put the Scholars to shame & silence many times, and they said; "how knoweth these men these thing's being UNLEARNED". Mans schools can not teach Gods mysteries. Fred found 90% of all the Last Day statements & writings, by scholars & Denominational Leaders to absolutely wrong. Bro. Fred is fair & shows everything the scholars say & what he says BOTH in this book. Christian's should double check what they been taught since their eternal life is at stake. Jesus warned many times; "Many false Prophets will come & deceive MANY". This Bro. Fred who refuses to be called Rev. is at peace standing alone with no human support while resting in the comfort of the "Comforter".